For Emily & Brent —

Enjoy the ride!!

Jay Steinfeld

JAY STEINFELD

Praise for *Lead from the Core*

"Jay Steinfeld's book is a must-read for business students, nascent entrepreneurs, or anyone who wants to expand their entrepreneurial mindset. The narrative of the book flows easily as the reader experiences both
the pitfalls and triumphs of entrepreneurship punctuated with lessons
learned and actionable takeaways."
— **Katie Pritchett, Ph.D., Former Director of the Entrepreneurship
Minor UT-Austin Faculty Member, Management Department**

"Ascending from the home garage to The Home Depot takes courage. It
also requires a spirit of generosity and a willingness to ask for help. Jay
experienced a life fraught with tragedy, sacrifice, disruption, rewards,
and success. His book offers a detailed chronicle that's jam-packed with
life lessons learned. Read it, reflect on it, and take these lessons to heart."
— **Leo Bottary, Founder/Managing Partner, Peernovation, LLC**

"This book's guidance on maximizing stakeholder relationships is
required reading for any startup founder thinking about raising growth
capital. Jay's specific advice on soliciting and leveraging advice from
board members should be used by entrepreneurs both young and old!"
— **Blair Garrou, Co-founder and Managing Partner,
Mercury Fund (startup venture capital)**

"Jay's educational lessons, insights, and philosophies have become an
integral part of my entrepreneurship curriculum. They resonate so
much with my graduate business students that he frequently gets standing ovations when he finishes speaking to them."
— **Al Danto, Entrepreneurship Faculty Jones Graduate School
of Business Rice University, #1 Graduate Entrepreneurship
Program (Princeton Review / *Entrepreneur* magazine)**

LEAD

FROM THE

CORE

LEAD
FROM THE
C O RE

THE 4 PRINCIPLES
FOR PROFIT
AND PROSPERITY

JAY STEINFELD

Matt Holt Books
An Imprint of BenBella Books, Inc.
Dallas, TX

BenBella Books, Inc.
10440 N. Central Expressway
Suite 800
Dallas, TX 75231
benbellabooks.com
Send feedback to feedback@benbellabooks.com

BenBella is a federally registered trademark.
Matt Holt and logo are trademarks of BenBella Books.

Printed in the United States of America
10 9 8 7 6 5 4 3 2 1

Library of Congress Control Number: 2021941583
ISBN 9781953295729
eISBN 9781637740064

Editing by Katie Dickman
Copyediting by Michael Fedison
Proofreading by Lisa Story and Cape Cod Compositors, Inc.
Indexing by WordCo
Text design and composition by PerfecType, Nashville, TN
Cover design by Brigid Pearson
Printed by Lake Book Manufacturing
Illustrations hand drawn by Joseph A. Galantino

To those who strive for impossible dreams. And to Barbara and Naomi, without whom I would never have achieved mine.

CONTENTS

Contents

BEFORE IT'S TOO LATE

Death destroys the man, but the
idea of death saves him.

—E. M. Forster

The phrase "core values," especially when used around an office, often doesn't elicit much excitement or interest. Indeed, core values are thought of as nothing words, as soft, squishy ideals created by the HR department to be put on a plaque, hung on a wall with no practical application, and never thought of again.

And that's how I thought about core values, too. Then my wife died.

On August 12, 2002, my wife, Naomi, died of breast cancer at the age of forty-seven. We'd been married for twenty-six years, and throughout that time had been partners in life as well as in business. Now, left to do it all alone with three children and a business still in its infancy, I faced a complete reevaluation of my life. Suddenly, I wasn't sure how to define happiness, or even whether I could ever be happy again. I thought often about what success meant to me, what it was that made me tick. I'd made it that far in life without ever really considering—at least not deeply— what truly *mattered*. Essentially, it was only when I found myself on a precipice that I asked myself: What are my core values?

Through intense introspection, what I discovered changed the trajectory of my life, and the trajectories of all the people *in* my life. In fact, it was only after understanding what these values were—the values that drive my behavior—that we were able to begin building a company of significance, a company that became the number one online retailer of blinds in the world.

My motivation was never to start a massive company—it's difficult to get very far if this is your only goal—but instead, to achieve as much as I could before I died. Looking back, I realized that death has always been my key motivator—it's been an unwelcome but consistent presence in my life for decades, ever since my mother, Elaine Steinfeld, passed away at forty-six from ovarian cancer. I was twenty, a junior in college, and she was my constant.

With her strong work ethic and drive, Mom took small jobs to keep our family above water. They were mostly secretarial, but she also sold jewelry she rescued from antique stores and her own decoupage art. What I unwittingly learned by watching her over the years no doubt played a large role in how comfortable I've always been with the pursuit and risks of business. I remember Mom coaching me how to raise money door-to-door for my little league team. She would coax me to a neighbor's door, then run around the corner, hiding, to *force* me to do it myself. Though it was the nonchalant, matter-of-fact manner in which she pursued risk that really struck me, and programmed me to accept risk as an everyday facet of life.

My dad, on the other hand, was a struggling salesman. Fred Steinfeld had great passion and optimism, professional artistic and musical talent (skills I later found in myself, though to a much lesser degree), but none of the same grit I respected so much in my mother. Mom told me quite specifically to *never* become a salesman. Of course, I ended up selling blinds.

That's a key difference between those who have built something significant and those who only dream: grit. A significant chasm opens up, separating those who *wish* for acclaim and success and those whose mantra is: *I will persevere to achieve my goal. Tirelessly.*

Another critical component of my success was the faith of those who knew me best. I have a vivid memory of driving away from the graveyard after laying my mother to rest. As we wound down the narrow cemetery road, I turned around in the back seat, looked back toward her grave, and said, "I know you believe in me. Don't worry, I won't let you down."

I felt the same when I lost my dad, and again when Naomi passed, both of whom had unwavering confidence in me. That strength and belief from those who know you best is immeasurably valuable in helping you take the risks necessary to grow, and it's important to find those people, to surround yourself with those people who support you. Entrepreneurs inevitably come up with ideas that others believe are unlikely, improbable, impossible, or even insane. In order to succeed, you need the friend who can tell you that to your face while at the same time cheering you on each crazy step of the way. When passion combines with the confidence gained from true friends and supporters, it buoys you to say, "I know it's improbable, but I'm going to experiment. I'm going to try this. I want to see how good I can become before I run out of time."

My appreciation for the scarcity of time heightened after I lost my Naomi. I was no longer a twenty-year-old kid with every possibility ahead of him. I had to think about how to motivate not only myself, but also our three children—Esther, Craig, and Alec—ages eighteen, sixteen, and eleven, respectively, at the time. How could I help them find a reason to keep going when the person they loved most in the world was gone? That was my challenge.

Profit and Prosper from the Core

Business has always been personal to me. I learned the value of grit from my mother. My father-in-law gave me my start in the corporate world. I shared my business with my wife, dad, and kids. More on all that later.

But nothing was as personal as when Naomi's health was declining rapidly, after she detected a lump in her breast. You never believe that it's going to be cancer, but it was. And when it *is* cancer, you never believe it's the kind that spreads, but Naomi's lumpectomy revealed it had already spread into her lymph nodes.

I remember being at the hospital when the surgeon came out. I'd already been pacing and waiting five hours, drinking cup after cup of bad coffee, both eager and dreading for the surgeon to reappear. I stood up, alone, when he told me. Then I fell to a chair, devastated. She passed away within five years of her diagnosis. My children will tell you I dove into work even more after she died, and they're right. At work, things made sense, had an order. I could control that world much more than I could the one at home.

I couldn't recognize any of that in the moment—when you're thrown for a loop like that, it's only in retrospect that patterns arise—but after Naomi's death, I was clearly trying to accomplish as much as I could before I, too, passed away, though I was perfectly healthy. I realized how brutally unfair and short life could be. There were times, too, when I allowed that grief to become anger and railed about the unfairness of losing the two women who meant so much to me so early in my life. Then came clarity. Their faith in me—my mother's and later Naomi's—fueled my passion to leave a legacy of kindness, of helping people achieve what they never thought they could, just as my mother and Naomi had done for me.

A few years after Naomi's death, when my frustration around the constant anxiety I felt was too disruptive to ignore, I began a practice of heightened introspection that I have kept up to this day. I sought the help of outside professionals, and at the same time began reading books on philosophy, happiness, and how people define success. Two books that particularly impacted me were *Man's Search for Meaning* by Viktor Frankl, and *The Happiness Hypothesis* by Jonathan Haidt. The first helped me to appreciate, and even illuminate, silver linings that emerge from tragedy, and the second gave me a framework to see how environment and other factors affect one's condition and behaviors.

Looking back now, I see that this was the beginning of a critical evolution for me. I faced many more challenges along the way, some seemingly trivial at the time, but each a key step in my personal development and eventually that of the company.

I put my beliefs into words that would later form the principles not only for the rest of my life, but also for a thriving business with an award-winning culture. That culture is what helped us grow and evolve as a business and as people, materially profiting as well as prospering in the more emotionally fulfilling, intangible sense. Over time, these became **the 4 Es**. They are also the foundational principles on which this book rests and will appear over and over again. While I'll highlight the many ways in which I've integrated **the 4 Es** into both my personal life and into my company so you can do the same, it's helpful to give a basic introduction to each here, a synopsis that you can return to throughout the book as needed:

1. **Evolve Continuously:** In my personal life, **Evolve Continuously** means actively seeking change and growth always, constantly being on the lookout for what more there is to learn and to improve upon, and what needs to be adjusted to adapt to whatever is thrown my way. In business, it's making sure that my employees are afforded these same opportunities, to enact change and to better themselves and their lives—whatever that means to them. So, whether in personal life or business, it's the deliberate intention of improving yourself and everyone and everything within your sphere of influence. It's one of the key reasons I've written this book—to help *you* evolve.

2. **Experiment Without Fear of Failure:** To experiment is to be cognizant of failure. If you expect to succeed—and do succeed—every time you try something new, then you're not experimenting, and it's detrimental to kid yourself that you are. Experimentation can be small—a new recipe for dinner, perhaps—or life-changingly, business-shiftingly large. In order to **Experiment Without Fear of Failure**, one must feel liberated to do so. It might mean that the calculated downside risk is small enough that failure is worth it. On a company-wide scale, however, when your employees feel supported in their freedom to experiment—and their freedom to fail—that's where things really take off. A leader who touts the freedom to experiment not only attracts like-minded employees, but *keeps* those innovative employees, too.

3. **Express Yourself:** We've been told to "express ourselves" since childhood, but oftentimes don't feel truly free to do so. If nothing else, consider this my permission to you to **Express Yourself** always. As a leader, your job is to protect your business and to protect your employees. If you're not able to express their needs

clearly and firmly, your entire company ethos is likely to suffer. In the workplace itself, your employees should feel comfortable and empowered to communicate with candor and respect, without fear of judgment—and they should *really* feel this. As a leader you are literally paying these people for their brainpower. Why not open yourself up to what they have to say? I have always held that the best answer wins, no matter who it comes from, and no matter how long they've been with the company.

4. **Enjoy the Ride:** Pure and simple, why do something if you're ultimately not enjoying it? Business is full of risks. Heck, *life* is full of risks. There's pressure, there's setback, there's indecision, and there's uncertainty. It could be hell if you let it be. It's why I'm always looking for that silver lining, the fun that lets me **Enjoy the Ride**. Take the time to notice when things are going well—and find the humor when they're not. Every failure is an opportunity to learn, and to laugh at how wrong something went. Competition is nothing but a game (or so I tell my genial nemeses!), and there's always room for improvement. Perseverance and grit will get you far, but if you're not enjoying it, then maybe it's time to try something else.

It's amazing how much better an organization can become, how much better *you* can become, and how everything you do is incredibly more impactful when you follow **the 4 Es**. Each has its own specific benefit, but I'm of the mindset that none can work as well without the others. These tiny, incremental changes, when done consistently, begin to compound, just as money compounds over time. Anyone can incorporate these values into their lives—both personal and business. You'll be surprised how often the opportunities show up when you're looking for them.

It was in Naomi's death that I learned how to define success. It's not how much wealth I could amass or how many people I employed or how much Home Depot paid to acquire my company. I define success as being constantly *in the process* of getting better and helping everyone around me get better than they ever dreamed possible. That's what drives me and why I returned every day for more than six years after I sold Global Custom Commerce to Home Depot in 2014.

I had 175 associates at the time, all of whom believed me when I said we weren't there to sell blinds. We were there to become better than we ever thought we could be.

And here's how we did it.

THE BEGINNING OF MAGIC
Why You Don't Need to Know Everything at the Start

It's the little details that are vital. Little things make big things happen.

—John Wooden

Like many entrepreneurs, I'd dreamed of owning a company for as long as I could remember. As a child, I imagined it would be a sporting goods store. In high school, I made custom T-shirts, which resulted in a reprimand by the principal when I started selling them on campus. And, to earn my way through college, I went door-to-door offering to paint street numbers on curbs for homeowners.

When it was time to decide what to study in college, I interviewed successful business owners before making a choice. I was already unwittingly demonstrating the behavior of speaking up—expressing myself. You'd be surprised what people will say yes to if you just ask. Each one said that, before anything else, I needed to understand financials and advised me to study accounting. I hated accounting. To me, counting other people's money is boring.

But I put my grit and determination to work and majored in accounting at the University of Texas at Austin. From there, I followed the logical career course and took a job as a CPA at Peat Marwick Mitchell, one of the big eight accounting firms at the time, now KPMG. I was employed, I was earning a living—but I knew I was not living up to my promise to my mother.

And I hated it, every single day. I was making $12,500 a year, which, in 1976, was a fairly good salary. It was a prestigious, plum job—I even wore a three-piece suit. But it was mundane, except maybe the day I was told to climb a fifty-foot ladder to reach the top of a giant industrial oil tank to check its volume, lightning striking in the distance.

After two excruciating years, I got my first big break, experimenting without fear before I even consciously knew what that was. Naomi and I had just gotten married, and my new father-in-law, Harold Nedell, was partnered with Sam Meineke. Back in 1972, they worked together to nationally franchise Meineke's five muffler repair shops, and by 1978 there were thirty-five franchised stores. When my father-in-law asked if I wanted to move to Houston to join Meineke Discount Mufflers as VP of finance, I jumped at the chance.

After successfully building the small chain into a franchise of over eight hundred stores, Harold and Sam were ready to diversify into other franchised businesses. Little did I know then that the idea of taking a platform, in this case franchising, and extending it to other products would become one of my powerful growth engines. Over the course of the next couple of years, we considered numerous options. First, we partnered with a couple who owned a retail gift store in California, but that never took off, so we decided not to franchise. Finally, in 1981, we partnered with a local blinds retailer and launched Amy Shutters in west Houston with Naomi at the helm, making in-home appointments and selling ready-made blinds inside the store.

Naomi and I had met in college at the University of Texas in 1973. I was a sophomore, and she was a freshman. I met her at a party on a Saturday night. We were both from the New Jersey–New York area, which set us apart in Austin, Texas. I took an instant liking to her—as did my roommate, Harry. When I got home that very night, Harry told me about this great girl he'd met at the party who he intended to ask out. Naomi.

I said, "Well, I'm sorry, but I've already asked her out."

I had not. There was no way I was going to miss my opportunity, though. The next day I called her, and the rest, as they say, was history. Naomi and I dated all the way through college. A few weeks after she graduated, we married on December 26, 1976.

By 1983, when I'd been working for Meineke for five years, they sold to Guest Keen and Nettlefolds (GKN), a global UK-based business. As the new owners were only interested in the auto business, GKN stopped the franchising activities. That was the end of Amy Shutters.

While I'd known the sale was coming, I had no idea what that meant for me. Just a few days before the deal closed, I discovered that the post-sale org chart, the diagram that shows everyone's name and the hierarchy of where they fit within the organization, did not include me.

I'd already earned and been promised a bonus of $150,000, and I became concerned that they would not pay me if I was fired. Not willing to let that happen, I took the documentation about my bonus that I had received from the president of the company, including notes in his handwriting, and put it in a safe deposit box. A few days later, I was brought into the office of another executive who was not my boss and told I had to leave the building immediately. I was, in fact, fired. The shame of that was bad enough, but it hurt even more that the coward to whom I reported didn't have the guts to do it himself.

Still, the experience taught me two valuable lessons. First, as difficult as it is to terminate someone, it's much more painful to be the one being terminated. Second, when you are the leader, as much as I assert that delegation is essential to growing your business, some things you never delegate, such as giving bad news. When you abdicate the tough parts of communication to others, everyone learns something about you that is not flattering and does not engender loyalty. Leadership does not mean being chickenshit.

I emotionally regrouped as best I could, then took a US marshal to the safe deposit box to witness that the bonus documentation had been placed inside ahead of time. Then, I hired the famed plaintiff's attorney Stephen Susman, who had founded the Susman Godfrey law firm and who took the case on contingency. I called the gutless president and told him what I had done. Days later, I got my bonus.

After I was fired, despite the advance notice and having taken action regarding my bonus payout, the rejection still stung. That afternoon, I sat at home, hugging Naomi, and we both cried. All decisions are difficult, those made for you even more so, but leaders push forward despite the pain.

Now, at age thirty-two, I had no recurring income and no job. I did some inconsistent consulting work, but it felt like I was on the sidelines and not in the game. With the birth of my daughter, my family was growing, and I needed something that was both reliable and that would feel like my unique talents were being put to good effort. I will never forget how difficult those days were and how frightened I felt being out of work without clear prospects. It's why I will always have empathy for anyone out of work and for young students bewildered by their next steps.

Harold, my father-in-law, had learned how to franchise during an earlier stint at AAMCO Transmissions, and told me that the transmission business was lucrative. Through a business broker, I submitted an offer to buy a successful, local, and privately owned transmission shop, Astro Transmissions. It wasn't that I saw a big future in transmissions, or even that I might create my own franchise. I saw it only as a means for stability and income. Anything further was not contemplated. I offered the owner's asking price, but he got cold feet and rejected my offer. This turned out to be lucky for me, though at the time I was demoralized. Only in retrospect have I learned that it's not important to get everything you think you want, especially if the reasons behind that want don't match up to your values. Many times, it's better that you don't, and you'll see numerous examples of that in this book.

The future I'd really wanted hadn't worked out, but in that empty space something new and unexpected emerged. Harold had begun franchising a business out of Arizona named Laura's Draperies, Bedspreads & More, founded by the Koenig family in 1937. Good at what he did, Harold soon had five company-owned stores, and in 1987 offered one to Naomi. Shortly thereafter, based on her success and my lack of income, I decided it was worth a try to operate a second one in Greater Houston's Clear Lake area. If my dream had always been to own my own business, why not experiment? Despite my lack of design knowledge and having no passion for interior design, this felt like a step in the right direction.

These were small mom-and-pop stores. Naomi was the mom, and I was the pop. We each became shop-at-home decorators helping customers in their homes, coming by with our vans full of samples and helping people decide which window coverings were best. I spent Monday through Saturday on appointments in Clear Lake, nearly an hour outside Houston, and every night and Sundays working the books.

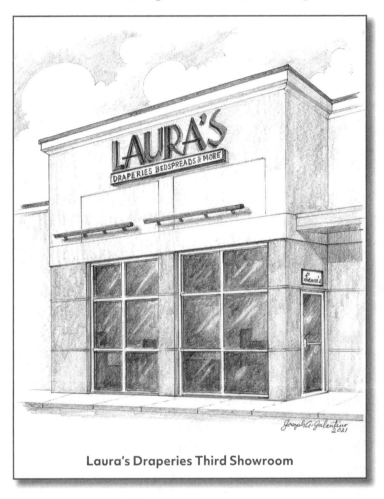

Laura's Draperies Third Showroom

When our third child, Alec, was born in 1990, Naomi decided to spend most of her time at home raising our children. To make this feasible, we consolidated, closing my store and keeping Naomi's, which was much more conveniently located near our home. I also invested more time in an idea to use the newly burgeoning internet as a sales platform.

That was 1993, the year before Amazon launched. I spent just as much time working that year as I had when we had both stores, but this time, I filled my hours focusing on my experiment: selling blinds on the World Wide Web, aka the Information Superhighway. It was an experiment no one at the time believed was possible.

That same year, when I needed to hire a new Laura's Draperies showroom manager, I called my dad. It had been nearly twenty years since my mother's death, and he was selling office signage and still living alone in Dallas. Dad had never been financially successful, though I had learned a great deal from him about how to care for those you love by watching the way he cared for my mom during her illness.

My brother and only sibling, Bobby Steinfeld, recalled to me on Father's Day 2020, "What I remember about Dad, of course, was his creativity and talent, but what stands out the most was how he was there for Mom when she was sick: taking care of her, providing emotional support and love to the very end."

Maybe, in retrospect, Dad did have grit in the things that matter most.

If you're a parent, you understand that sometimes you frustrate your children. And not just because you tell a "dad joke" or interminably play the same old '70s rock songs. I know I sometimes say to my three children things that come off as insensitive. And other times, I don't always take them seriously when they need it. I know, too, that my behavior was always more attuned with the business than with the family. Hopefully, one day, I'll be granted some leniency like the way I now view my own dad.

In 1993, I asked Dad if he wanted to move to Houston to help me. It took some cajoling, but eventually he did and it was a mitzvah, a blessing, boosting his self-esteem and bringing us the closest we had been since I was a kid. Every day I watched him proudly support both the business and me with his customary enthusiasm. Turns out he really could sell, after all. Dad's job was to answer the phone and work with prospective customers who entered the showroom, and to set up appointments for me and the other shop-at-home decorators we employed from time to time. I didn't know it at the time, but not long after, Dad would get extremely sick and pass away, just one year before Naomi died. His being there in Houston, nearby for his final years, was a blessing indeed for us both.

You'd Be Surprised!

Back in 1993, I never envisioned the business becoming the world's largest e-commerce site for window coverings. Who would? Buying online was nearly unheard of at the time.

More than that, though, I did not yet consciously understand my core values. My goals were solely to provide for my family and feed my desire to create something I could grow. Just *starting* is one of the most daunting decisions you'll likely make when you begin in business, especially when you have an opportunity to take or keep a job with a salary and benefits. But, through the internet, I saw a way to create the scale and growth for which I had always hungered.

I maintained the traditional storefront with Laura's Draperies, and kept visiting people's homes, measuring their windows, and delivering custom blinds. On the side, however, for just $15, I acquired the web domain name Lauras.com. When I went online in 1993 with Lauras.com, it was a low-risk $1,500 marketing experiment designed with the sole aim of generating leads and creating the impression that Laura's was progressive and current with the latest in design trends. In actuality, the website didn't sell a thing. There was no business plan and no research to determine market size or market fit (i.e., whether enough customers will even buy your products). All I knew was that the market was being inundated with mail order companies, not to mention mega retailers like Home Depot, and we small guys needed to do something to stand apart. At that time, Home Depot and its ilk weren't yet online, and so there was my opportunity.

The most ironic thing about this is that, just over two decades later, Home Depot would pay handsomely for the very company their early success and lack of investment in the Web helped create.

But that was all in the future. Back in the mid-nineties, three years after the Lauras.com test, I launched a real effort to sell blinds online. In 1996, I spent $3,000 to create the all-online company NoBrainerBlinds .com. I was forty-three, but I was still naive to think people would figure out which blinds matched their needs, measure their own windows, choose colors and fabrics without seeing or touching samples; and install the blinds themselves. Had I been more sophisticated, or possibly more formally trained, I would have hired a consultancy and conducted customer surveys and analyses that would have shown clearly that this was a fool's errand. It was many years before I realized how much my naivete turned out to be an advantage.

I remember precisely where I was standing when I told Naomi, who was sitting in the Laura's showroom at the time, that if we were going to make buying blinds a no-brainer, why not call it NoBrainerBlinds.com? Then, I quickly drew a head with no brain, filling in the face with brains instead. It was disgusting, but I liked it, and that was that.

Andy Rachleff, cofounder of legendary venture capital (VC) fund Benchmark Capital and a professor at Stanford University, espouses the idea that business must be right and have *no consensus*, meaning your idea must be a good one, and few, if any, others also must believe it to be so.

NoBrainerBlinds.com fits Rachleff's description perfectly. *I* knew it could work, but no one else thought so—a customer survey analysis

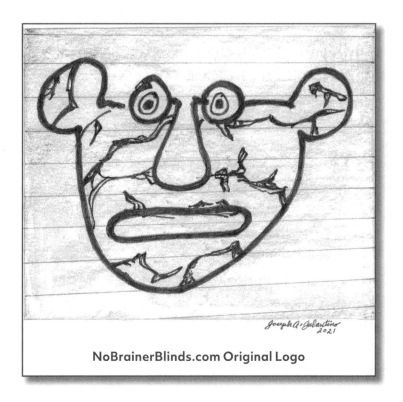

NoBrainerBlinds.com Original Logo

would have proven that. The market for blinds online was nonexistent. The market for *most* things online was nonexistent. The do-it-yourself (DIY) market paled at less than 5 percent of the size of the do-it-for-me (DIFM) market, the latter of which Laura's Draperies was a part. That meant there was no interest from anyone else, which gave me ample time to grow slowly, with little investment and little knowledge.

I was running the company at first out of an office over the garage of our home, but no one else had to know that. I wanted to project professionalism and, thinking big, I changed our address to One Brainer Tower. Years later, at a national conference, I ran into Maurice Nieman, founder of our competitor, BlindsGalore.com. He asked me how large the tower was. I answered honestly: "You'd be surprised."

One Brainer Tower

All Our Customer Service Representatives Are Busy

Guess what? It worked. I sold custom blinds without setting foot inside a customer's home. Over the phone from my van, I helped people measure their windows. I saved them significant money and myself a tremendous amount of overhead. With no employees to pay and no ads to budget for, the only overhead was the $35 monthly web hosting fee.

The NoBrainerBlinds calls went to a separate line at the Laura's desk, where the showroom manager answered. She'd tell prospective customers, "All our Customer Service representatives are busy. I'll have one call you back," before calling me on my car telephone, which was the size of a brick. The first call I ever received came in while I was on the highway, driving past the Summit. At the time, it was where the Houston Rockets played, but it has since been converted into Joel

Osteen's Lakewood Church. Half-excited, and half in disbelief that this venture might actually work, I pulled off the highway, called the customer back, and made my first sale from the outside shoulder. Picture alongside me my price catalog, order pad, ten-key calculator, and the brick of a phone resting on my shoulder as cars zoomed past and you've just about got it.

After a year, enough calls were coming in to put Naomi on the phones, taking them off the Laura's desk. Naomi was a great salesperson, always had been. She was full of energy, and customers loved her. Throughout all of this, mind you, I still maintained my typical day at the brick-and-mortar Laura's Draperies, with two to four in-home consultations each day, which generated my family's income.

NoBrainerBlinds was in its formative stage, but growing, and soon I needed help. I ran an ad for a designer and hired Ann Werner. Ann was cheerful, experienced, and one of the sweetest people who's ever worked with me. That was the good news. The unfortunate news was that not long after Ann came on board, Naomi became unable to work due to cancer treatments.

I knew it was up to me to manage and grow both businesses, and to take care of my family and sick wife. Looking back, I'm not sure how I got through it all emotionally. It's mostly a blur, though they say that happens with grief. Perhaps I convinced myself Naomi's diagnosis wasn't as serious as it was. Maybe I realized the only things I could control or affect were the businesses and so zeroed in on those. I couldn't change what was happening inside Naomi. I couldn't forever shield our children from the devastation barreling toward them. I couldn't protect any of the people I loved from what was happening.

But I could use my grit and talents to create something wonderful and new, and so that's where my energy went. The online business was ramping up and we were on top of each other, outgrowing our space. The small showroom for Laura's Draperies was 1,001 square feet. It had one desk and a couple of tables for customer consultations. When I needed to make my second hire for NoBrainerBlinds, Sharon Scheckter, we had officially run out of room.

Sharon is from South Africa, which you can detect the second she speaks. I was worried that her accent would be difficult for people to understand, and voiced this concern to Naomi. Naomi overruled me, and I'm glad she did. Even though Sharon was a teacher with no design background or sales experience, she was open to learning, and I believe she cared even more about customers than I did. Sharon later supervised our Customer Service department and eventually led all cultural aspects of our company, a position to which she was perfectly suited. My first two hires for NoBrainerBlinds were gambles, and both were some of the best decisions I ever made.

An Alley Only a Rat Could Love

Next to the Laura's showroom was a kitchen remodeling store with an available back room, which they subleased to us. It was a boon to have our expansion space so close by, but there was a catch (of course). The kitchen remodeling store didn't want us walking in and out of their space to access the back room, which meant that we had to go halfway around the block and into the alley behind it to enter the office from the rear. It was a hassle, especially when it was raining.

The office had no windows, which might have been a blessing given the stench of the dumpster from the nearby Chinese restaurant. The space was only about eight hundred square feet, and poor Ann and Sharon felt claustrophobic in there without windows. It was a constant battle between opening the door for fresh air and the odor they suffered when they did.

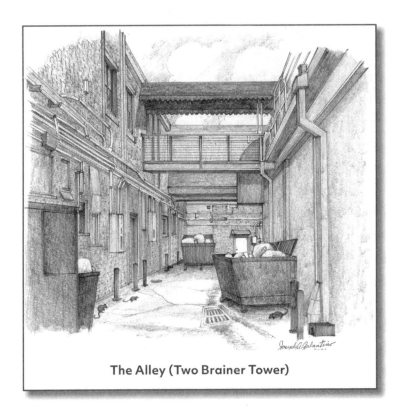

The Alley (Two Brainer Tower)

Our former part-time accountant, Marilynne Franks (Bleeker), remembers it well: "That's where I would have to go to exchange the financial information. Sometimes I couldn't take it. Ann put a blind on the solid door and pretended it was a window."

Marilynne suffered through The Alley days and stayed fifteen years until she retired, along the way donning many hats. As the business grew, so did her responsibilities, in the same manner in which Ann and Sharon progressed.

"As the vision and company grew, my role grew and changed, until I first converted to a part-time employee and finally a full-time controller," she said. "Jay allowed my job to evolve at my pace and as my personal situation changed."

Despite those early working conditions, both of my first two hires were still with the company when I retired in 2020 (actually, re-*wired*, but more on that later), reflective of the low turnover rate of 8 percent that I was proud to maintain throughout my career.

"Back when I first started, twenty-two years ago, I knew we had something special," said Sharon. "I knew this was something that was going to become bigger than it was, and watching the company grow and change, it's been an amazing ride. If I had to leave, I would retire. I don't think I could go anywhere else."

Ann remembers how important values were to me from the beginning: "Jay said, 'Always do the right thing,' even from the very beginning when there was no money. You can imagine with Naomi being sick with cancer how much that took, but no matter what, he did the right thing."

Thinking big was innate in my associates from the very beginning.

"We took phone calls for sales and service, and if anybody would call and want a manager, either Ann was my manager or I was her manager," Sharon remembered, laughing. "We always wanted to appear larger than we were."

Of course, we named the alley office *Two Brainer Tower.*

Within five years, with just Ann and Sharon, NoBrainer was generating as much revenue as Laura's, and it ultimately became the site where the world's largest e-commerce blinds company took root. When we first launched, we dubbed ourselves "The World's Most Popular and Trusted Online Site for Blinds!" Being that we were the only e-commerce blinds site, it was true. The words you choose and how you choose to use them can make a huge difference in how you appear to potential customers. We puffed ourselves up often in this way to appear more credible.

It's hard to believe that in those first five years, we spent nothing on marketing, and pay-per-click advertising had not yet begun. Google didn't even exist. Instead, we relied on guerilla marketing. We used social media in part, though that term had not yet been coined. Several times a day, I'd visit what were then called bulletin boards—forums today—where people posted questions about blinds and home improvement. Whenever a question came up relating to blinds, I'd answer it, leaving behind my signature as CEO/founder of NoBrainerBlinds.com, with an easy-to-remember phone number, 1-888-4NO-BRAINER.

We also learned about search engine optimization (SEO), from possibly the only search engine expert who existed at the time, Danny Sullivan. Danny did all the SEO himself, and because of the novelty, we were atop every major search engine, including AltaVista, Excite, HotBot, Lycos, and Yahoo. Besides developing content and refining meta tags within your website's code, it was customary then to get as many reciprocal links to your site as possible to show your popularity. We spent a lot of time scouting for those, even buying some if necessary. Danny now has become one of the world's foremost experts on SEO.

Besides Danny, whom I've still never met in person, there was a small group of other experts I found through web searches. To me, each appeared to be the best in their field—at least as far as I could tell at the time. Turns out, they were, and twenty-five years later are rightfully recognized as such: Eric Ward for PR, Nick Usborne for copywriting, and Jim Sterne for web conversion and optimization. Each provided their seasoned expertise, and it was at this point where I began to sense the importance of teams.

With only Ann and Sharon handling the phones and no money in the budget, I needed to find more ways to get in front of more people and build their trust in us. I used banner ads, but not in the way you might think. I did not pay to place ads on other websites to link back to NoBrainerBlinds. Instead, I stuck ads for *other* companies such as ProFlowers and FedEx, on *our* site, with no outbound links. The purpose was solely to create the illusion that these formidable companies had paid to be on NoBrainerBlinds, and thereby boost our credibility.

We made QuickTime videos to demonstrate how to install products, something no other company was doing. Instructional videos were still things you bought physical copies of in 2001—YouTube had barely launched. Still small and scrappy, I found a local videographer to come to my home and film me installing the blinds. I paid $500 for him to film, edit, produce, and do a voice-over narration of the instructions for three how-to videos, each about twelve seconds long. I still watch them from time to time for amusement. In case you're up for some cheap entertainment, visit my website JaySteinfeld.com and see them yourself.

I also added testimonials. I got that idea from mail order catalogs, which were replete with them. Since mine was a fledgling business, testimonials were hard to come by, so I made them up. They were obvious fakes, don't worry. NoBrainer gathered reviews from Paul Bunyan, Abraham Lincoln, John Kennedy, and twenty others, all created by a local impersonator voicing clever puns these luminaries might have said. I cannot tell you it boosted sales, but it amused me. I was **Enjoying the Ride**.

The tone of the NoBrainer website was based on the NPR radio show *Car Talk*. *Car Talk* was a call-in show with two smart MIT graduates, Tom and Ray Magliozzi, who owned a car repair shop in Boston (their "*fair city*"). Irreverent and hilarious, the brothers adeptly answered questions about cars, jabbed jokes at each other, and added in playful tidbits of life philosophy. That's how I viewed NoBrainer. Each week, *CarTalk* listeners were asked to solve a puzzle and send their answers to Puzzler Tower—hence where I got the idea to call my home One Brainer Tower. When you're looking for ideas to grow your business, look far beyond your direct competition. You should learn from every business, every ad you see, and every person you meet. Everything is inspiration. Everyone is your mentor.

What I believe set us apart from competitors as they arose, and hundreds eventually did, was that our business started as a brick-and-mortar shop. That meant we saw our customers every day, talked to them, and therefore knew them and the kinds of questions they were asking. We knew that if any one customer had a bad experience, our whole reputation could be tarnished. We believed that we were actually providing *better* service online than we could do face-to-face, because we used technology and speed to service them. Ann, Sharon, and I were true blinds experts who deeply cared about satisfying everyone.

That should always be the driver of lifetime value: customers' satisfaction with your product and service, and the value you provide.

You Stink

It wasn't only The Alley that stunk. For all our cute ideas, NoBrainer Blinds.com, as a website, was barely viable. There's a term that originated in the technology process agile development, referred to as *Minimum Viable Product* (MVP). Instead of creating a full-featured, fully developed product, you create a version of the product with just enough features to satisfy early customers, which will provide feedback for future development. It's also a way to establish an overall direction without knowing exactly how everything is going to look or be built. You establish MVPs so you can advance the customers' usage of the product before it's perfected. The main benefit is you don't spend too much time creating detailed specification documents, because by the time you do, the market and customers will have changed, along with technology, rendering what you've built obsolete. Plus, by allowing customers to use your product, you get great feedback on what the market wants instead of having to guess.

In our case, MVP might be too generous a descriptor. Better, I think, is HVP: *Hardly* Viable Product.

Our technology was inferior at best. I have never been a technology expert, just someone who knew what technology could accomplish. I'm less *high-tech* and more *high-touch*. The first website required customers to type in the names of products they wanted to buy and enter the prices themselves, based on what we listed on a grid. They'd then have to also tally up the prices themselves and type in a credit card number—or print their whole order out and mail it, along with a check, to One Brainer Tower. People were still afraid to use credit cards on the Web, and barely anyone had broadband, so it took a long time to load pages. Back then, our goal was to load the home page in under thirty seconds. Now, if your page takes over four seconds to load, you might as well close up shop.

I probably don't even have to say that order confirmations were not automatic. At the end of the day, I'd see the two or three orders that had come through and send all the confirmations at once. For each, I manually typed each customer's name into a template, then emailed it myself. Can you imagine ordering during the day and not getting your confirmation until that night, and thinking nothing was wrong?

In 2001, when our competitor Joe Mehm, owner of BlindsWholesale .com in St. Augustine, Florida, sent around an email offering to sell his business, I jumped at the chance to triple down. Revenue at NoBrainer was already up to $1.5 million. But Joe was outpacing me, selling $3 million online, from his home. I did my due diligence, hired a CPA from a large regional accounting firm run by a fraternity brother of mine, Rick Stein, and we traveled to Florida. We stayed at Joe's home.

All looked good, so I began the process of raising money. Rick introduced me to one of the most respected and successful entrepreneurs and philanthropists in Houston, Jim McIngvale, founder of Gallery Furniture. Mattress Mac, as he is affectionately called, agreed to provide all the seed capital, almost $1 million, in return for 51 percent ownership. A couple of weeks later, however, the deal fell apart when Mac's IT guy told him that our technology was horrible. Which, as I've already written, it was.

Still, with an excellent financial opportunity available and my future at stake, I worried about how I might raise the $900,000 still needed to buy BlindsWholesale. I was in no position to fund any portion of it myself. What even made it seem feasible was that I had raised money before (for a failed business that I'll explain later). Having gone through that experience made it easier to ask, as did having a solid business opportunity attached to it. In the end, I raised $500,000 from local friends and a regional blinds manufacturer. It was far short of what I needed, but Joe was still game for the sale. Together, he and I convinced his blinds vendors to allow me to defer payments for ninety days. After about five months, we had no debt and I still controlled the company with 60 percent ownership.

In retrospect, we were lucky the deal with Mac never happened. I'd have hated not to have the controlling ownership in the company or to have deprioritized blinds on behalf of furniture.

Others may be smarter, but when they think too much, you act. The acquisition of BlindsWholesale.com was my first of several. Your ability to creatively use a small amount of capital to do something much bigger is a crucial trait shared by many entrepreneurs. Whenever you can pull it off, you are better positioned later to secure institutional investors and much larger amounts. When individuals give you money, they want you to squeeze out every penny. It's a specific trait that comforts investors—as it should. John Doerr of Kleiner Perkins defines entrepreneurs as "people who do more than anyone believes possible, by using less money than anyone believes they need."

6 WAYS TO LAUNCH A BUSINESS WITHOUT MUCH MONEY OR KNOWLEDGE

1. Accept the fact that no one is clairvoyant, and that you seldom, if ever, have 100 percent of all the data you need to decide. Just start.
2. If you wait until you have all the information, by the time you start, the information will be outdated.
3. A pad and pencil can work just as well as a sophisticated spreadsheet, especially at first.
4. A solution does not need to scale at first. It's OK to throw away the minimal work you did to prove out the solution. Better that than to build a fully developed system only to discover that there's no benefit to anyone.
5. Hire outside consultants versus full-time employees for those roles that require expertise far beyond your own. Keep their stints short and well defined.
6. Consider your lack of funding as a potential benefit—a gift—because having too much money risks people getting lazy and not thinking about more efficient ways to solve problems.

HAIL TO THE LIGHT BULB

*How to Experiment Without
Fear of Failure*

*Our greatest weakness lies in giving up. The most certain
way to succeed is always to try just one more time.*

—Thomas Edison

Along with the BlindsWholesale purchase came the right to use the name Blinds.com. At first, we set it up as merely a website redirect, meaning that if people entered "blinds.com" into their browsers, then mainly Netscape Navigator and the emerging Microsoft Explorer, they would end up on BlindsWholesale.com. Some ten thousand people a month were going to Blinds.com and landing on our website, which cost us $3,000 a month for that right. It was a great deal at thirty cents per visitor, and also a great indicator of how our customers were finding us.

After a few months of this, we decided Blinds.com should be its own company and website, but didn't want to start a website on a domain name that we were, in effect, renting. We basically had a land lease for the name with no assurance we'd be able to keep it, and we didn't think it was a good decision to build on rented property. So, I made a deal with James Katz, the owner of the domain name. I agreed to pay $350,000 over seven years with no interest—it was an experiment banking on the idea that people would type the simplest thing possible into their browsers, and another example of how scrappy I learned to be with money. Though, being scrappy is an experiment of sorts in and of itself. One might think that the easiest path to success is being able to throw money at everything right from the start, but I disagree.

Over the years, the company continued to grow—by 2001 we had fifteen employees and had outgrown The Alley for a more traditional office space—but for a moment, my personal life came to a standstill. Naomi, who had been beside me every step of the way, and had pushed me to make decisions I would value for the rest of my life, passed away. The confluence of growing a business with all its inherent responsibilities, along with the need to be both a father and stand-in mother, took a toll on me. I rushed into marriage soon after Naomi's death, which turned out to be one of the worst decisions of my life, and the marriage ended shortly thereafter. In its wake, however, it proved deleterious to my children's lives. It was all happening too soon—they needed more time to grieve and more time with me. Part of me must have known that, though I thought I was making the right decisions. But what I didn't realize until many years later was that I'd also needed time with *them*. Even today, nearly two decades later, we still suffer from the ramifications of not being together then to develop into a more emotionally cohesive family.

It was also during this time, in the years just after Naomi's death, that I went on a cruise to Alaska with my kids. That's when I began that period of introspection I referenced in the first chapter of this book. I looked inward, and I looked deeply, and out of that came an inkling of what would eventually become my **4 Es. Evolve Continuously. Experiment Without Fear of Failure. Express Yourself. Enjoy the Ride**.

By far, the core value that resonates the loudest within our halls is **Experiment Without Fear of Failure**. I'm of the belief that in this era of extreme accountability and immediate finger-pointing, the freedom to make mistakes is intoxicating.

Don't get me wrong. People are still accountable for results. The accountability is that they must explain what they've learned and embrace the failure as an opportunity to improve continuously. I don't believe another core value, **Evolve Continuously**, can exist without it.

Getting better means trying new things, and that can be uncomfortable. Experimentation means being comfortable with not getting everything perfect every time—and, sometimes, even making things worse. As the leader, you must be OK with that and, most importantly, let everyone else know it applies to them, too.

I've made many mistakes, such as wrong hires, keeping poor performers too long, giving ambiguous instructions, allocating capital to the wrong project, ineffective marketing, and so forth. When asked whether there are any decisions I wish I'd never made, though, I take a more philosophical view. The simple answer is "no." Just one decision made differently might have changed where the company ended up, where I ended up, so I think it best not to look back.

What's in a Name Matters

While my tenure at Meineke ended less than amicably, franchising taught me how to replicate a recipe, and then leverage it to scale. I learned that platforms are one way to grow without changing your business model. We'd gone from NoBrainerBlinds to Blinds.com, which had already brought us thousands of customers who might not otherwise have found us. I was eager to see what more we could do.

Dr. Peter H. Diamandis, who is an international pioneer in the fields of innovation and commercial space, owns multiple businesses and is founder and chairman of XPRIZE, which catalyzes global impact to solve some of the world's most daunting and complex challenges, wrote in his book *Bold* that the best way to create a billion-dollar business is to help a billion people. To even be able to reach a billion people, let alone help them, a business needs to build a scalable platform. Many of the best businesses with the highest valuations are themselves scalable platforms, like Facebook, Snapchat, and Twitter.

We first tried to extend our platform by appealing to decorators and designers, but this was 2003, and they had yet to form an affinity for technology. Still, we were sure it would work, and spent over $100,000 to hire an outside firm to build the technology as a white-label solution. That seemed like a fortune at the time, and our investors thought we were insane. The bad news was that they were right. The decorators and designers never ended up buying much from that website. Technically, this might be called a failed experiment (as some experiments must be), but the good news was that the technology we built became the launching pad for our next big thing.

Throughout the years and transitions the company went through, I've always tried to think about the next step. No matter what crossed our path, I stayed focused on the vision that we could become more than we thought possible. Beyond growth potential, diversifying also protects your business if the original product becomes obsolete (I've always worried about the development of some technology, like a film or new type of glass that obviates the need for blinds). So, we looked at the platform we had built, the technology and consumer data we had collected, and thought we would be able to use it to sell in other custom, hard-to-buy categories. We thought about doing custom sofas, custom tables and chairs, and home irrigation systems. No idea was a bad idea at this stage.

Thinking big prompted us to change our legal name to reflect this broader vision. We decided to rebrand from Blinds Acquisition LLC, a nondescript name given to us by our attorney, to something that would reflect our long-term potential and what the vision of the company became. No longer was I the guy in the van, walking people through their own window measurements. We weren't even just a window coverings retail company. We had more to offer. Although this would largely be an internal branding change, it was critical in helping our associates understand our full potential. Words matter and sharing my vision mattered, which is why I invited our associates to help create our new name. One of their suggestions was Custom Commerce, so I added "Global," and within two days, it was official. We were Global Custom Commerce, Inc., or GCC for short. We were going to provide worldwide manufacturers the opportunity to sell in North America without any physical presence, using our technology.

Building with Builders

Basing your corporate culture upon **Experiment Without Fear of Failure** allows you to attract entrepreneurial associates. Getting them involved—no matter where they fall in terms of experience or hierarchy—in big decisions, like what to rebrand your company, proves to them that you mean it. In fact, you'll find, I tend to avoid a hierarchical structure as much as possible.

Looking slightly ahead for an example, in 2007, I hired an independent consultant named Steve Riddell to advise us on how to make our folks on the phones more effective. One year later, I asked him to stay permanently. At first, he declined, citing concerns that he was not good in a traditional employment setting. However, our culture of experimentation won him over, and he stayed until 2015, making GCC the place he was employed longest at one time in his lengthy career.

"He does value **Experiment Without the Fear of Failure**. And that, to me, was a good sign that at least I got a shot at being entrepreneurial within a company environment," Riddell said. "And I think that's what helps with any kind of growth in any company."

Along with my vision for our future, the culture of experimentation is part of what attracted Seth Todd to join the company when we recruited him away from Home Depot (ironically), where he was the Director of Strategy for Online Support.

"He wants to make a difference; he wants to have an impact. And that's part of what drew me down here," Seth said. "But, if I'm honest, it was also that I wanted to do something different. I wanted to start my own business. This is a bunch of entrepreneurs, a bunch of people who did something amazing on a small scale. They all just got a buyout—I'm going to learn anything I can about how to do this."

Over the years, I have seen hundreds of associates take chances and achieve things they never would have if they weren't encouraged to do so. From writing books to opening their own businesses, GCC associates are among the most entrepreneurial you will find.

Take sales coach Lance Fisher, for example, who was twenty-one and working at Starbucks when he joined GCC. Now, he's thirty-two, married with children, and says the core values radically changed the direction of his life: "I developed in numerous roles throughout the company. I was given the opportunity to co-create our Health and Wellness Program, become certified by the International Association of Coaches, and co-create and deliver our very first internal coaching certification program."

John Suh, a designer and developer with GCC, told me, "I live my life by testing without the fear of failing and made it my mantra personally and professionally. When things aren't working, we step back and try another creative solution until we get positive results." John and his wife, Christine, have recently launched their own restaurant.

Allowing people to experiment helps us determine the right fit for them in our company structure, regardless of the job they were initially hired to do. Many of our associates have changed roles and even departments at least once and many multiple times. If we have the right person, we experiment with the role until we find where they can flourish and contribute the most.

As I've hinted at already, it's not enough to say you *encourage* experimenting without fear. You have to really mean it, and your practices have to demonstrate it. One way we did that at GCC was visually. For me, the physical office environment embodies corporate culture. At GCC, you will see each of our four core values represented frequently and literally throughout our space.

To testify how important experimentation is in our culture, I set up two six-foot-tall, clear test tubes in a prominent area of the office. In one were clear marbles. These represented experiments, things associates had tried, but that didn't work. In the other were dark marbles. These represented successes. I was beyond proud when, after a few months, the tube of clear marbles vastly outnumbered the tube of dark marbles. For us, the success was in trying.

When something goes wrong, how do others react? How do you react? Are some punitive? Retaliatory? Or do you work to understand, learn, and move forward?

"The unforgivable sin is lying or hiding stuff. Not screwing up," said Daniel Cotlar, who was the Chief Marketing Officer for GCC and the first C-level officer I hired. "You make a mistake, OK, we'll figure it out. If you repeatedly make mistakes, you're probably in the wrong role. Let's figure that out. There were people here who failed in a few places, and Jay moved them around."

Many companies believe moving a failing associate around delays the inevitable, but I hire for culture and fit. Individuals who fit our culture are diamonds, and it's my job and the job of my leaders to find the right setting for these diamonds.

"Jay's very much about the right seat on the bus," Daniel said. "At one holiday party, he gave out these little school buses, and it was all about being in the right seat on the bus and we can find that for you because we're all on the bus together. Jay loves to see people figure things out. He loves seeing people succeed."

Many of our associates either wanted to start a business, or already had one on the side. An interesting pattern among my leadership team is how many of them didn't want to work for a big company or never wanted to do the same thing for very long. Yet many of them stayed with us well beyond what they had expected.

"I've stayed here and done this for five years, because I think the things that we've decided to do are worth staying with a big company and trying to make happen," Seth said after I'd pulled him from managing thousands for Home Depot to head up a team of just forty for us.

Despite the fact that I have operated a single company for twenty-four years, I consider myself a serial entrepreneur. As Seth Godin, the legendary marketer, wrote in his blog about businesses coming under new management, "If you think about it, every day, *every* store is under new management, if we define 'new' to mean we learned from what happened yesterday."

Every day, my business evolved, and every day I evolved. Therefore, I ran a new business every day. New businesses create ever-changing opportunities. Nothing gets stagnant, including ideas and people. People often leave companies due to a bad supervisor or because they get bored. With a new business every day, work is never boring. The only people who leave that type of business, assuming they're reasonably compensated and did not leave due to extenuating circumstances, are those who cannot keep up.

Measure Your Mindset

When you experiment for the purpose of evolving (which combines two of our core values into one), you need enough data to understand the results. Truly fostering a culture that supports experimentation comes from establishing honesty and trust. Much of this can be achieved by how you communicate to your team.

First, it's important to note the difference between formal and informal experimentation. Both start with a hypothesis, but *informal experimentation* relies on an agile work environment and experimental mindset. For instance, you present to your associates your hypothesis, such as the idea that compensation should be quantified on a tiered system. You then admit outwardly that you don't know if what you have landed on is structured right, no matter how many scenarios your financial analysts have modeled. That shows vulnerability and encourages the buy-in from your audience, whether that's your associates or a leadership group. Whatever the makeup, you've now established that everyone is in it together in the effort to **Evolve Continuously**. That way, when the inevitable unexpected consequences occur, and you must course correct, people are more likely to accept it. It's for the team as a whole—not just for you.

If you don't create this mindset of experimentation, people will only do what you tell them to. And if all they do is what you tell them to, they're not coming up with their own ideas. Since they're the ones actually doing the work, they're more likely to come up with better ideas than you. Without this mindset, you're killing innovation in your company.

It's critical when something goes wrong—and it will—to keep your cool. Ask your associate what their hypothesis was. What assumptions did they make, and which turned out to be true and which turned out to be false? What did they learn? This not only helps create the mindset you want, but it also helps you understand which individuals can be trusted with more responsibility. You'll learn who went into the experiment with a plausible hypothesis and reasonable assumptions and who started panicking the second something went wrong. It also trains your associates to think like problem solvers and holistically like owners. Remember, you're building evolving leaders, not hatching lemmings.

With *formal experimentation*, it's all about the metrics. You start with multiple brainstorming meetings, where together you develop a list of perhaps hundreds of hypotheses. It could be about what you think would increase conversion rates, what might yield higher order sizes, improve customer satisfaction, boost repeat and referral business, and so forth—whatever goal you're trying to achieve. Then you add to that list the benefit, cost, complexity, and time of completion for each hypothesis.

Finally, you prioritize the list and experiment as fast as you can top to bottom. Jeff Holden, former chief product officer of Uber, calls this method "furious experimentation." I believe a telltale sign of an organization's health is the rate at which it experiments. In order to have the ability to experiment as much as possible, your company requires a process, structure, and methodology, which should be conducted at a consistent and never-ending cadence.

Your company should constantly be asking questions, building hypotheses, testing, learning, and analyzing results. You should be comfortable with your experiments failing perhaps at a higher rate than they succeed, especially at first. Through this constant and furious experimentation, you learn how to ask better questions and you get better and more comfortable at experimenting over time.

If you don't experiment, you keep doing the same thing, and throwing more money at the same thing. Not only is that boring, but it's not a good way to scale. It's not a good way to make more money. It's not a good way to learn. It's certainly *not* **Enjoying the Ride**. You *must* experiment and you *must* expect things not to go perfectly, because they never do.

WHY PEOPLE WON'T EXPERIMENT

1. People fear getting fired if the experiment doesn't work.
2. They are incentivized and rewarded for doing other things.
3. Even with a successful experiment, there's not enough financial or career upside.
4. They have been trained to do only as they've been told.
5. It is an incorrect assumption that you must in advance know and solve every conceivable angle of what might go wrong. Yes, you should always think of potential adverse ramifications, but don't let them prevent you from trying something small.
6. They do not have a consistent process to determine which experiments to try.
7. People do not have an adequate baseline of how something is now working or the analytical ability to measure any improvement.
8. They do not have the time to do anything more than what they've been assigned.

HOW TO EXPERIMENT AND ENJOY THE RIDE

1. Try something tiny at home, not at work, to flex your experiment muscles.
2. If your overall corporate culture is to be risk averse, try something only in your department or work pod within your department. Tell your supervisor you're trying it and be sure not to let it go too long without monitoring the results. Do not hide the results—good or bad. You must be transparent.
3. There are no sacred cows. Everything is on the table to evolve. You and everything your business and you do are never as good as they can be.
4. Small, incremental improvements compound over time, especially when done furiously.
5. When supporting your grand vision or combating an existential threat, existing or anticipated, prioritize your experiments and never cease experimenting.
6. Think of experiments as a game. Have fun. Enjoy the ride!

After all of that, it might surprise you to know I'm actually quite risk averse. You'll never see me gambling because the odds are inherently against me, no matter what system I deploy. In determining when and how to experiment, I think about *downside risk*. If that downside risk is acceptable, I move forward. If not, no matter the odds, I will not risk sinking the ship. Experimenting without fear is not about being fearless. It's about having nothing, in fact, to fear.

And . . . We're Off, or Maybe Not

As the newly minted Global Custom Commerce (even if the only people who knew about the name change were our lawyers and employees), we were on a roll by the mid-2000s. I'd impressed upon our team how our core values were the basis of our company culture, but the best way to lead is, of course, by example, and so I was eager to continue to evolve— and hopefully never stop.

With that foundation, it was time to get more aggressive with our growth. So, I pursued our second acquisition. In 2005, JustBlinds.com was outpacing us in revenue and profit, especially the latter. I admired Kyle Cox, the founder, for the organization he'd built and was dumbfounded by (and competitively jealous of) his success. I had to have in.

We met a couple of times for lunch at an Olive Garden restaurant located midway between each of our offices, coincidentally and fortuitously both located in Houston. I pitched my offer to buy JustBlinds. Kyle and I came to terms, and, after closing the transaction, we boosted our revenue overnight from $15 million to $33 million. Kyle's staff consisted of many of his family members, including his mother, Karla, who was a stellar performer on the phone selling blinds. I kept everyone on because I was sure they'd be able to teach me how they'd performed so well. Besides the improved cash flow that our combination brought, we now had the critical mass to afford hiring more senior people and to develop systems and technology that could be leveraged across both businesses. I credit the acquisition of JustBlinds.com as being a pivotal accelerant of our growth.

I also credit that acquisition with illuminating for me what now seems obvious. Kyle had hired Jamie Bragg as his Director of Operations, and so with the acquisition of JustBlinds came Jamie. Though Jamie left us less than a year later to join Men's Wearhouse (later called Tailored

Brands) and eventually became its Chief Supply Chain Officer & EVP, his impact was significant. That year, Jamie, Daniel, and I were thinking about our holiday schedule, a seemingly innocuous topic—but not to Jamie. Jamie's first thoughts were about phone messaging, scheduling, workforce optimization, technology integration with our suppliers, and how it might affect all our systems. Sheesh, why didn't I think like that? Eventually I learned not just to think conceptually about growth, but to understand that the nuts and bolts were equally, if not more, important. So much for me to learn!

Along with Kyle Cox, Maurice Nieman (the founder of BlindsGalore .com who was once impressed with the size of One Brainer Tower) was a formidable competitor, and I considered both my nemeses. You have to remember that, in the early 2000s, digital advertising was still in its infancy and we were all scrambling to try anything we could. Banner ads, as ineffective as they might be, represented a large component of what companies were doing. And forget about computer-assisted campaigns, or *programmatic advertising*, as it's now called, that help streamline and optimize your campaigns across platforms.

For example, pay-per-click (PPC) advertising is where advertisers pay other websites, Google especially, a fee each time one of their ads is clicked. Essentially, it's a way of buying visits to your site, and one of the most popular forms of search engine advertising. It allows advertisers to *bid* for ad placement in a search engine's sponsored links when someone searches a keyword related to their business offering (e.g., blinds, car insurance, best car wash soap, etc.). The larger your bid, the higher and more conspicuous your ad would be, and the more likely someone would click on that ad, bringing them to your website.

Before Google made PPC advertising the ubiquitous mainstay of digital advertising, there was GoTo, which later became Overture. Kyle, Maurice, and I had running battles on GoTo, manually changing our bids every day, several times throughout the day. Kyle would jump to number one, then I'd wake up in the morning and hop to my computer and bid a penny more. Then Maurice, not satisfied to be in the third position, would leap ahead of me, spiraling up the cost of our bids until one of us realized our foolishness in bidding so high and jumped back to third place. But—and this is the important part—we would still bid just a penny over the fourth-place bidder. There were Kyle and I bidding outrageous, out-of-control amounts while Maurice sat comfortably with lower bids, albeit bringing in less traffic due to the third-place ranking.

I don't think any of us really knew what the hell we were doing. I know I didn't. I certainly had no analytics to help me make data-driven decisions. All I knew was that we each despised being beaten by the others. In retrospect, I think we each probably enjoyed the competition and the camaraderie. In some strange way, battling with competitors was kind of fun and another way to **Enjoy the Ride**.

Sales continued to grow until 2008, when the economy collapsed. Our revenue, then hovering around $45 million, flattened for two years—the only time in our history when it wasn't growing. What saved us was our decision to continue experimenting and growing with agility. Because of this, our profits increased. Maintaining an increase of profit in a time of nationwide financial instability comes with its own challenges, of course, and we had to carefully watch our expenses. That included labor costs.

For the first time, but not the last, we had to make difficult decisions to eliminate positions. While it's easier to use phrases such as "eliminate positions" or "decrease head count" than "terminate people," unless you have a stone heart, letting people go is tough—one of the toughest things you'll do. When you eliminate many people at the same time, sometimes referred to as a reorganization (or *reorg*)—another of those phrases that makes the process less personal—it's tougher in some ways and easier in others. Eliminating many at once elicits company-wide fear that there's something significantly wrong with the business, but also means one's termination is less indicative of any one individual's performance. We cut eight of our approximately fifty associates that year, so it was a hefty percentage.

I was a rookie at this business of firing, so I began, as usual, researching best practices, particularly around how to keep panic and uncertainty to a minimum. What resonated for me was something I applied whenever I had to announce bad news of any sort. I'd try to think of all the questions people were thinking, especially those they'd be afraid to ask. It's a good practice to get a lot of help from your team on this. Then, I'd make the announcement as succinctly as possible and dive right into going through each question before anyone had a chance to ask. I'd tick them off one by one, not leaving anything sensitive off the list. One last suggestion: before you tell your whole team, it can be helpful to first tell privately a few key employee influencers and get their feedback on the news, because they'll probably have some additional questions none of you had anticipated. Consider this a form of customer feedback. Allowing your employees to **Express Themselves** helps everyone.

A couple of examples in this case were: "Are there going to be any more people let go?" and "Why were these people in particular chosen?" This transparency helped build trust among the associates whom we kept on, especially in difficult times. Admittedly, these are tough questions and there are legal considerations as to what you can and cannot say. So, tread lightly.

We continued training our people throughout the financial crisis and continued to experiment and organically grow our culture. We invested in marketing and new advertising platforms. There was never a day when we slowed down out of fear of what might be. We saw the potential for the future and never stopped running toward it.

Breaking Up Is Hard to Do

The times when you have to eliminate multiple positions due to market challenges or other circumstances are, hopefully, rare. However, letting go of poor performers when things are otherwise going well is a much more common issue for leaders.

The memory of my time with Meineke and my feelings about the boss who didn't even have the courtesy to fire me, his direct report, in person fueled my desire to never be that person. Really. Don't be that person. While it may seem contrary, the act of letting someone go who can't get the job done is a generous one. When someone is let go for poor performance, it's usually not a surprise, at least not deep down. Likely, they're mired in a problematic position where, for whatever reason, they can't meet expectations and are suffering. Caught in a cycle, they either don't see a reasonable way out, or they do but can't face it themselves.

Here's the toughest part of facing this challenge: these are often not typical poor performers. I'm not talking about people who willfully and chronically underperform, who show up late consistently or refuse to grow. Not the people who just don't care. Those souls are easy to identify and should be exited as soon as possible.

The more difficult exit is someone who has been great, who has been loyal, and who got the company to where it is now but will not be able to get it where it needs to go. They've got the right attitude. They share the core values. They may even want to change but are unable to do so at all or quickly enough. If you allow such people to linger, the company will suffer, you will suffer, and everyone around you will suffer. Over time, the other employees will look to you, see your lack of action, then begin to question your leadership. And while it may feel harsh, they're right to do so.

As you consistently mind the gaps in your company, this requires honest scrutiny of individuals. Are they where they need to be? If not, can they get there? If so, how fast? And are they open to change? You try to see the gaps coming before they are upon you, to maintain your growth momentum. But seeing them in people you have relied on, who have been loyal to you and the organization—this is very difficult.

Start by laying the groundwork openly and honestly. Make it a clearly stated fact that people must grow with the company. Of course, that doesn't eliminate the issue. I have looked in the eyes of many people over the course of my career who truly wanted to be able to do the job ahead of them, who wanted to grow into the evolving role, but who would never be able to get there—at least not without another several years of development. In those cases, I had to make the hard decision and let them go, or, if available, move them to a position where they could continue to excel.

In many cases, as the company grew, I needed to add higher-level experience and expertise—C-suite positions—where taking a chance just on personality and grit doesn't always work. It meant hiring someone into a position above an existing leader. That's the decision that led me to Larry Hack. The person who was leading IT at the time was doing a good job and had been with us for several years, but he wasn't an expert in the structural, methodical way one needs to build software. And neither was I—yet I was relying on him to have our technology developed in an efficient way that could solve our customers' needs and help us grow. After many months of obvious starts and stops, it was getting harder to tell my investors that we had a good handle on our tech, because we didn't, not anymore. I couldn't rely on our head of IT to continue on in his current position.

Counterintuitively, though, we had hired right. Many might have opted to rid themselves of what appeared to be a bad hire, but Larry, whom I brought on in 2007, understood the need for change and how it would benefit the company and mission we shared. Larry handled the situation expertly, sensitively seeking the displaced IT associate's feedback and integrating him into his own process, providing ample opportunity for him to grow in areas more suitable to his experience and preferences. He accepted Larry's leadership despite having himself been the leader up to that point, and remains with the company today. He's one of the most valuable associates we have because, by now, he knows so much about everything and can therefore solve problems no one else can. This happened countless times with associates over the years. But I must confess, while I had no compunction about doing it, each time I had to make a people move like this, I dreaded it.

Finally, there's a third type of performance challenge you must deal with quickly, or it will negatively impact your company: the person who is a top performer, but does not share your core values. These are the folks who might be doing everything "right," and who are, for all intents and purposes, excelling as far as the numbers might show, but who are not a cultural fit. Ultimately, having someone like this on staff is toxic to your company and everything you're working to build.

Some years ago, we had to fire one of our best salespeople because she was antagonistic with customers from time to time—enough that it got noticed. She was one of the first ten sales associates we'd ever hired, and knew better. My sales manager labored over the decision to let her go and the impact it might have on our revenue. But, conversely, keeping her on the team told everyone that bad behavior in misalignment with our core values was acceptable as long as you were doing well in other places. It never is. It can't be. One day I was told she was gone. The decision had been made. The right decision.

Keeping any of these three types of underperformers is unfair to the associates who are working hard, doing a good job, and who truly support the company's culture and core values. If an associate is not fulfilling the expectations of their job, others are either picking up their slack or worrying about negative consequences despite their efforts to grow the company.

And, as a leader, it's an obvious weakness that can cause anxiety among your team. The assumption is that you're either so obtuse and disengaged you don't see the issue, in which case your best associates will wonder how you could possibly miss something so troubling, or that you're afraid to face the conflict—and if you can't deal with this common leadership issue, how can you handle more complicated ones?

I admit I've taken too long to make all of these decisions at various points in time, and have heard stories galore about other entrepreneurs who've done the same. Maybe it's the inner optimism inherent in entrepreneurs. Once the decisions are made, however, it's almost certain you'll say to yourself, "How did I let it go so long?"

Make Your Path the Autobahn

As GCC grew, we realized the e-commerce platform we'd been operating on had a significant gap that, until filled, would neither allow us to continue our rate of growth nor make us appealing to an acquirer. We had already made the difficult decision to close NoBrainerBlinds.com in favor of the simpler Blinds.com. We hadn't been fertilizing NoBrainer, and the fields were becoming fallow—traffic was falling, so we decided to close it.

It was a sad day, but a necessary one. People thought I was going to resist it, but I really didn't. It had to be done. As the leader of a business, you're going to feel the pain of difficult decisions as much as anyone. You have to make them regardless.

We also closed BlindsWholesale.com, our first acquisition—another nostalgic end of an era. Each of these websites consumed a certain amount of money, time, and mindshare that just wasn't worth it. Most importantly, we couldn't find a way for our customers to differentiate between them all.

That left us with what we called *B3*: JustBlinds.com, Blinds.com, and Blinds.ca, the last of which we created in 2008 for the Canadian market. Our gap was an unsettling growth inhibitor: all three sites operated on different technology platforms. Having multiple technology platforms is a formidable technical and operating problem. For example, improvements had to be made separately on all three sites. And bugs fixed on one site still remained on the others.

But these difficulties didn't keep us from allowing these separate sites to exist. For us, the thinking was this: generate sales, make money, then fix the underlying issues so you can scale and make more money. Big companies hardly ever think that way. Instead, they look for perfect, enterprise-worthy solutions and, by the time they model and get approvals, they've missed out on months and sometimes years of generating income and getting a head start on the competition, learning, and then evolving.

One of the reasons I hired Larry Hack to lead technology was to get his insight on purchasing a new platform to use for all three sites. Because it was his job, Larry spent six months assessing multiple vendors. What he landed on sounded complicated and expensive—a combination of WebSphere from IBM and a configurator company product that would cost us $1.5 million. It was far from ideal, but we decided as a leadership team to move forward.

Without my knowledge or go-ahead, however, Larry began having second thoughts of his own and then did exactly what I had actually hired him and all my executives to do. He questioned our decision.

In addition to doing what he'd been asked to do, Larry had *also* decided to write up a three-year total cost of ownership for all the related websites and maintenance over that time frame. It came out to

$4 million to $5 million over three years. When Larry presented his concerns and research to the leadership team, I understood, although I'm not a technical person, that our customized system was *part* of our secret sauce. Always had been. It had a tremendous value that we would give up by adopting an off-the-shelf product. We'd never get a third party to adapt quickly enough to our requirements—or to experiment with new features we'd want.

We also discussed how an expensive and integral relationship with third-party vendors could interfere with an acquisition should an appealing offer come in. We made our short-term decisions with long-term views.

When I asked him about this later, Larry recalled: "We all said, 'I think it's going to be better if we have our own system so if we go public or we get acquired, we're not tethered to anything.'"

Making the decision to create our own platform turned out to be the easiest and fastest part of the process. Larry spent the next two years creating Autobahn (originally referred to as *V2*), along with Tim Coonfield, one of our wizard engineers at the time and head of IT at GCC when I left.

While Larry and Tim were at work on what would become Autobahn, a chasm grew in our tech team. We couldn't just ditch our aging system while building the new one, and so managing the legacy system fell to the original team members. They assumed the mantle of maintaining the old—which created delays for the new, further separating them from Larry's new hires working on the exciting future of our company, Autobahn.

I meant it when I said that a name can change everything. Slogging away on the old system didn't feel great to one side of the team, so we renamed the existing system "Cash Cow." It was, after all, providing our way of life. As fit our culture, we showed gratitude for the contributions that helped us succeed. We gave each person a custom patch for their shirt.

Cash Cow / Autobahn Patch for Home Depot Apron

"It helped," Larry remembered. "We had these really talented people who were worried for their jobs, but the cool thing is they started improving Cash Cow. And it got better and better. And a lot of the things that we said we needed the new system for, because the old system couldn't do it, well, all of a sudden, now it does."

The plan had always been to switch over to Autobahn once it could do everything Cash Cow could, but as the team improved the legacy system, it suddenly became a moving target, getting ever harder to top.

IT folks commonly refer to that as "we keep moving the goalposts." So, we brought in a consultant to advise us. He told Larry the new system was destined to fail. In his experience, building new systems to compete with legacy systems always failed, so he advised us to abandon Autobahn and focus all our efforts on improving Cash Cow.

"I took the information to the senior leadership team, and we had this late afternoon meeting that stretched into the early evening that stretched into the not-so-early evening. Even I was waffling," Larry said. "I was brought in to build a new platform and . . . I'm even beginning to think maybe we should just enhance the legacy [i.e., existing] system."

I watched my team of incredible thinkers become paralyzed with indecision, considering how much money we were burning through working on dual systems. The advice of a consultant who did not know us and was not part of our culture weighed heavily on them. But still. "It never works," he had said.

Larry, who had been so strong in his conviction that we should build Autobahn, began to lose confidence. After hours of debate and self-doubt, I did one of the things you have to do from time to time as a leader. I believed in my team more than they believed in themselves.

I walked into an open area where the IT team was having their marathon meeting about which direction we should head. I stepped in.

"Enough," I said. "We're doing it. Of course, we're doing it."

Five minutes later, I walked out, and that was the end of the discussion. Eighteen months later, Autobahn was built, and not long after, Lowe's and Home Depot came calling.

Uh-Oh . . . Now What?

Experimenting without fear also allows you to become a disrupter, which is critical to growth. By doing things no one is doing, or doing them differently and better—creating your own independent platform, for one—you uniquely solve someone's pain.

I have always trusted my gut when it came to opportunities to disrupt. Ideally, my gut comes with a large side of data to support it, but that's not always the case. It's that quality that Steve Riddell—our one-year consultant who stayed for nearly eight years—believes gave GCC an entrepreneurial advantage.

"Jay was one that early on saw value in things that other people didn't see," Steve said, looking back on his years with GCC. "I remember going into his office and Twitter was just coming to be, and he was tweeting. I said, 'Jay, why don't you concentrate on something that's going to help the business rather than tweeting? I mean, what a waste of time.'

"He goes, 'Don't underestimate the power of social media.'"

I actually remember this moment exactly, because a couple of weeks later, that tweet earned me an all-expense-paid trip to Las Vegas to be the keynote speaker in front of thousands of people at an ice cream distributor convention. The tweet? A simple note of my admiration for ice cream truck drivers as the epitome of entrepreneurs.

When you see a trend, it's always better to jump in than simply read about it. Firsthand knowledge is key for learning and leading. Many people wouldn't have thought blinds over the internet would work, but you have to believe in yourself, trust your gut, and then seek the information to validate or negate your belief.

There's a trick that works well. When faced with what seems like an insurmountable problem, ask yourself, "What would have to be true for this to happen?" Then, based on your answer, ask it again, and again, and again, until you find a solution that's small enough to bite off and makes the outcome seem feasible. For instance, back at Laura's early on, we found that most people were hesitant to buy blinds because they were afraid to do the measurements themselves. What would have to be true to cause people to be unafraid? What if they didn't have to measure? What if they could just take a picture of their window and text it to us? What if we could take that picture and automatically use technology to determine the size of their window? What would have to be true? Machine learning. I couldn't have gotten to that answer if I'd stuck with the first question, but shrunk further and further down: bam.

I'm not always right about my disruptive ideas or always right at the right time. No one is, of course, but it's helpful to give an example of how I was once disastrously wrong. Yep, this is that story I hinted at earlier on, when I was detailing my campaign to raise the money to purchase BlindsWholesale.com.

Back in 2000, I'd successfully found funding for an online virtual gift basket operation I dubbed Giftgoodies. Always interested in diversifying where possible, I had a good feeling about this one.

Major Houston investors came on board, including some names you'd likely know, and I raised a seed round of $750,000 in about two months. With that seed money to show for my efforts, I was able to find a venture capital firm in California willing to put up $5 million to launch the business.

Then the tech bubble burst, the deal fell apart, and all the seed investors and I lost our money. A good idea—bad timing.

Losing my own money was one thing; I could handle that. More problematic was that some of those investors were my friends. I was embarrassed and ashamed. Sure, we all knew startups are risky, but I had to face a lot of people I cared about. You might call that failure, and it was in many ways. My investors obviously thought so. Looking back, I think I did a particularly bad job communicating to them as things were crashing down. I regret a lot about those times.

Years later, however, I found a silver lining in my experience with Giftgoodies. Through this ultimate failure, I learned how to raise capital effectively and how to paint a vision. That experience proved valuable time and time again over the years. So, don't be disappointed with lack of accomplishment. Not getting what you set out to get might be the best thing that's ever happened to you. This is the sort of lesson that's difficult to accept when something goes wrong, but there's a way to allay the anguish. Make a list of all the things you wanted to do, but couldn't. Then see how life might have turned out for the better. I've made a list of scores of such examples. If any one of them had resulted otherwise, it's likely we'd never have built a company worthy to be sold to Home Depot, and you'd not now be reading this book.

The bursting of the tech bubble and my failure to launch Giftgoodies was also concurrent with Naomi's chemo treatments. She was fighting for her life while I was fighting for the business we'd just begun to build together. Naomi, true to form, was concerned I would spend too much time with her at treatments, away from the business. She implored that I keep working to make money, so she would not have to worry about our family's finances on top of everything else.

Thankfully, friends stepped in to take her back and forth from treatments, and stayed with her as much as they could. But I worried plenty—about Naomi, our kids, the business, and the growing recognition that I might soon be doing all this alone. In retrospect, I can see now that even with Naomi alive, I was, in fact, alone. The decisions I made in the years after her death—both for myself and for my children—were based in part on my not wanting to be alone anymore, and needing someone to take care of *me* for a change. Some of those decisions I regret, but as with any bad turn, there's something to gain by looking back.

During the turmoil that followed the Giftgoodies debacle, several private equity funds made us offers to fund GCC's growth with minority investments. In 2006, we almost sold GCC outright to a public company that owned and operated many successful, well-known e-commerce companies. We used an investment banker referred to us by one of my early seed investors, and I thought we were going to close, which everyone believed to be a few weeks away. Then, we were told that the president of one of the acquirer's subsidiaries, who would have had us under her purview, had decided not to approve the deal. With that, it instantly fell apart. Another of the many accomplishments not to be. And another of the many not-to-bes that ended up a blessing in disguise. The price that company offered was one-sixth what Home Depot would pay for us later, though it certainly seemed like a good deal at the time.

Giftgoodies is also the business that brought me Daniel Cotlar, whom I consider a cofounder at GCC and instrumental in crafting the business into what it became. Another silver lining.

"That's a generous description," Daniel said when I relayed to him this perspective. "I graduated business school in 2000, and it was the age of startups. I was enamored with startups, which I still am. Jay had found venture capitalists who were going to fund him and was doing all the standard startup stuff. And he hired me, and I went to work for Jay in this little executive suites office. I think we built one of the first viral marketing models, which figures out if this many people pass an offer to that many friends and they take advantage of it—a financial model for how quickly something would spread. I heard somebody describing that ten years later—they thought they invented it."

And then the dot-com bust happened.

Daniel continued, "It became clear, we were going to have to wind this down. It started to disintegrate at the same time Jay's wife was sick.

So I saw him as his company was falling apart, and his wife was sick. In Yiddish, we have this word *mensch*. *Mensch* is an upstanding, good person: how somebody is when everything is against them.

"He tried to find work for me, while I was looking for another job. He needed help with his blinds business. In the back of the shop, he was doing some online business. But I found another startup—it lasted a year, and then it collapsed. And then I went to work for a large company for five years—Reliant Energy. But we stayed in touch throughout the whole thing. And then Naomi passed away."

Keeping in touch with Daniel was a blessing. I had three grieving kids and was myself personally decimated, all while our business was finally starting to thrive. True, it gave me something to channel all my grief and energy into, something I could control and steer toward a successful conclusion. But I needed help.

"Jay called me and said things were really starting to move. He was in the process of buying JustBlinds.com. All of a sudden, he hit critical mass," said Daniel. "People thought I was crazy, because I was leaving a nice solid company. I had just been promoted. But I joined, and I never looked back. It was amazing from the very beginning."

Trust Me, Trust Matters

Daniel and I worked incredibly well together and grew the company quickly. I knew I could trust him, and for me, trust is paramount.

As Stephen M. R. Covey wrote in *The Speed of Trust*, business goes much faster when you trust people. If you don't, then you've got to spend time checking on them or putting controls in place. Once you get to the point where you can't trust someone, then you must let them go. It's that simple.

To build trust in your team, start them on smaller projects. When they do well, give them more. It's that simple.

Whenever we had an important new project, I always sat in on meetings in the beginning. Mostly, I observed: How are they thinking, what is their mandate, what are their objectives, what are the dynamics in the room? I watched for who was leading—were they getting input from other people; were they railroading? As you grow to trust the group, and as you trust the people in it, you can—and should—gradually wean yourself from them. Before you know it, they're doing everything, and you don't have to spend any time on it. And then you delegate more and more, so you're not responsible for *doing* anything. You're just responsible for getting the right people—people you know you can trust—to do everything. As a leader you *must* stop trying to do everything yourself. Instead, admit and accept your gaps and find individuals to fill them. It was the ability to find top talent that took our business from a small startup to a nationally recognized leader in e-commerce.

When I realized that is when I realized what it meant to be a leader.

With that breakthrough, I was finally able to focus on what I really loved: growing people. I didn't have to worry about accomplishing the day-to-day. I trusted that my team was doing the right things that were in the best interest of the organization.

Trust goes both ways. If your team doesn't trust you to live your own core values, they're not going to live them either. If you just *say* they should feel free to speak up, but they don't trust that you're actually going to allow them to speak up and experiment without fear, they won't do it. They've got to trust you as a leader, that what you say is what you're going to do, that what you espouse is what you really mean and how you will act and what your behaviors will be. It is absolutely critical.

Finally, associates must trust each other. If they don't, then they start covering themselves. They document and memorialize evidence of conversations. When people cover their asses instead of their to-do lists, productivity and morale plummet. Demonstrate your trustworthiness authentically all the time and expect nothing less of your team, because a company that runs on trust is a company that can withstand all manner of setback, upset, and disagreement. It allows a company to grow bigger than might have seemed possible at first—and to weather the inevitable pitfalls.

GET REAL

The Power and Pitfalls of Growth

*Destiny is a name often given in retrospect to
choices that had dramatic consequences.*

—J.K. Rowling

When we changed our name to Global Custom Commerce from Blinds Acquisition LLC, it was an optimistic first step toward the ultimate goals of diversifying, growing, and extending our reach beyond the window-treatment market.

We realized the first step in achieving that dream in 2009, though in a slightly different form than our initial grand vision. Instead of moving into adjacent product categories, we partnered with Sears and Wayfair. The idea occurred to me when reading David G. Thomson's *Blueprint to a Billion*, specifically the chapter entitled, "Leverage Big Brother Alliances for Breaking into New Markets."

Thomson writes that big companies cannot create on their own everything they need to grow, and small companies need alliances with bigger companies to capture new customers and markets. He calls them Big Brother/Little Brother Alliances. At the time, our main concern at GCC was that our reach was limited online. Partnerships with large companies would allow us to reach their audiences easily and quickly. Ultimately, we did this by offering a white-label arrangement and creating our private label products to be sold at Sears and Wayfair. By partnering with these large companies, suddenly our reach became national.

"We created this idea of running a store behind the scenes. It was done with the goal of one day being the supplier for a Lowe's or Home Depot or JCPenney," Daniel Cotlar remembered.

"We started with Rugs Direct and Lamps Plus. Then Sears was interviewing people to do their blinds business on their website. And they did a perfunctory interview with us . . . but really, they were just trying to prove they had talked to one other supplier. They were going to go with one of the brands, Levolor, to do it.

"But we made a strong case, and we got the deal. It was a really hard win, but it positioned us that we could answer the phone on behalf of anyone, we could run their website, we could ship on their behalf. Based on the success of Sears, we partnered with Wayfair. And then our hunt was on."

"We sell over $500 million of home products annually online," Niraj Shah, founder and CEO of Wayfair, said of the deal. "Although we dislike outsourcing, we realized partnering with Global Custom Commerce was the right solution given the platform they created." Ooh, did you hear that, Larry? The *platform* we created!

Soon, we extended our reach to include Office Depot and Build .com. None of those relationships had actually generated much revenue, but they had proven our ability to develop technology suitable for large-enterprise public companies, which is what gave Home Depot confidence that we could write software and integrate it quickly into a company like theirs. When we made the decision to white-label, we didn't do detailed financial modeling. We just knew that the strategic implications were enormous and that a few hundred thousand dollars of cost over three months was a small asymmetric risk, irrespective of how much revenue we'd gain. There was little to lose, which allowed us to **Experiment Without Fear.**

And that helped us eventually sell the company.

Then Came the Bullies

Your goal in business is to make money. When you're small, nobody cares about you. But when you're successful, be prepared for the big dogs to take notice and come after you.

For us, that was the biggest blinds manufacturer in the country, Hunter Douglas. Though they were a supplier of ours, we suspected they'd always been wary of us. Even in our infancy, before we became the big disrupter in the blinds industry, their marketing manager simply refused to talk to me or answer my emails. Imagine that: we were one of their biggest customers, and they wouldn't speak to the CEO of the company. The bulk of their customers were mom-and-pop blinds retailers, and when we came on the scene, the internet was a newfangled channel most were just beginning to understand and few were fond of. We were pesky and disruptive, and their small retailer customers complained to them about us.

Why? We were competing with their customers in a way they likely perceived as unfair. They didn't like that our prices were low, and later we heard that they'd supposedly been telling people we didn't provide good service. In fact, we believed we gave at least as good if not better service than the mom-and-pops. Rumors were also circulating that we were selling seconds, or factory rejects, and customers would never get their money back if they had an issue with our blinds. Another falsehood.

We continued buying from them despite the tension because at the time their goodwill and name recognition was better than ours, so customers would start their search looking for the Hunter Douglas brand and then hopefully find it with us. We were still finding our way toward developing the Blinds.com brand, or so we thought.

Eventually, Hunter Douglas decided to just stop selling to online players such as us. We received minimal notice, and then they were gone. A move like that might have harmed us, but remember, we were used to—and good at—**Evolving Continuously**. We quickly started merchandising other national brands that competed with Hunter Douglas, and in the end, our business did not suffer at all. Even better, we made a higher margin on other brands, which resulted in us not losing a beat in sales, and made us more money. We learned that the preponderance of customers cared more about *where* they bought their blinds—and the *experience* they had during the process—than they did about the brand they were buying.

Soon, however, one of our other major suppliers, Prestige Window Fashions, ceased operations, causing us to have hundreds of unfilled orders and hundreds of unsatisfied customers making thousands of angry phone calls. That was a tough road, but we plowed through it.

Our Customer Service team was always determined and had been trained to solve customers' problems. Our systems were not equipped to handle the disruptive demand, but our associates' mindset and skills were. (Another point to hiring for culture fit and personality—had our Customer Service team not lived **the 4 Es**, I don't know that we would have made it through quite as well.) We worked a lot of overtime and brought associates from our sales team to help. Though they were not trained to efficiently handle such calls, we thought it was better to have anyone answer a call than to have customers on hold waiting what would seem to them like forever. When customers are frustrated, every minute counts. It also seemed entirely counter to our culture of helping if we were available to sell products to new prospects when existing customers (those who had already given and trusted us with their money) were kept waiting. Doesn't that irk you when it's easier to reach a salesperson than someone who can provide you with assistance for an order you've already made?

Competing with formidable competitors such as Hunter Douglas, Lowe's, Amazon, and, dare I say, Home Depot was easy because I was naive. I was too ignorant to understand how large and consequential any of them were, which was a blessing because it allowed me to focus on growth and not fear. Keep your eyes on the competition, but your focus on your own path.

It wasn't just our competitors that took notice. There was a time when *patent trolls* (also referred to as patent *sharks*) bared their sharp teeth, determined to bring us down, along with any other conspicuous e-commerce players they could get. Their game was to gain access to patents without any intention of using them, except to sue others for alleged infringement. Companies would either have to defend the suit, spending significant money, or cough up a settlement amount to make them go away. We took a firm stand against the trolls, but in a few cases the threat was easier to dismiss when the settlement amount was minimal. Some of the team thought on the basis of principle alone we shouldn't have paid anything. While I often understand an idealistic perspective, sometimes you must set aside your ideals for a more pragmatic solution. That's what the trolls count on.

Our burgeoning prominence also made us targets for people whose political views did not align with those of radio hosts with shows on stations where our ads ran. It got so bad that I wrote an article asserting we had no political affiliation, that we merely wanted to reach large audiences, which was true. In an effort for balance, we also advertised in places where the return on investment was poor, but knew that at least we were spreading our money among diverse constituencies.

That didn't silence the critics, who were mostly on Twitter, where many critics are these days, anonymously calling me and the company horrible names. That lasted a few weeks, then died down, which is mild in comparison to the hateful things said in public about others. Whenever I witness such hateful chatter, I recall my own experience and empathize how difficult it must be for those in the crossfire.

Becoming better known did have many upsides, however. Namely, and most important, sales improved. Less important, but more amusing to me, is the one week in 2010 when we appeared both in the White House blog (due to our increased hiring in a down market) and *The Onion* (the spoof cited Blinds.com's enormous demand as the reason the internet crashed). Maybe it's odd, but I'm particularly stoked about the reference in *The Onion*.

Being part of pop culture is cool! I've got both articles framed together and displayed proudly in the office, though I'm probably the only person who gives it such significance. For me, it was a way to celebrate and **Enjoy the Ride**, and that created a form of propulsion to boost me through harder times. Whenever you find these flickers of joy in business (and in life), I think, it's good for your psyche and all those around you.

With a Single Step

Through tenacity, we got bigger, and it became easier to compete. It never occurred to me that anyone would one day consider *us* big bullies, perhaps because we always thought about our competitors respectfully. Where we had opportunities to make acquisitions, we did, but we always treated the companies and their people with utmost respect.

We were the same way with our suppliers. We never lied; we never bluffed. We just did what was best for the customer. As Ann said, we always did the right thing.

To think big is one thing. There are many people with vision. To execute effectively is another, and it requires patience and strategy. You have to be willing to start small and work hard to grow your idea. I believe that much of my own success comes from just doing a bit more than any rational, typical person might do. Stick out just a bit and people notice, and eventually, someone pivotal notices. In the meantime, while you're consistently and patiently performing, you have peace of mind that you're doing your best. John Wooden, considered by many to be the greatest basketball coach of all time, won ten national NCAA championships in a twelve-year period, with a record seven national championships in a row. In other words, he did a lot of winning. Yet his definition of success is "peace of mind that is the direct result of self-satisfaction in knowing you did your best to become the best that you are capable of becoming."

James Clear, who wrote the book *Atomic Habits*, once tweeted, "Act fast on things that compound. Never let a day pass without doing something that will benefit you in a decade. Long-term thinking is not slow acting."

And because this point is so key, I feel compelled to give you one more example, this time paraphrased from Lin-Manuel Miranda's character Alexander Hamilton: "[Act] like you're running out of time."

The Road to $100 Million Began in Detroit

One of our most influential acquisitions came in 2010 (the year of *The Onion* article, fortuitously, though I'll admit they probably had nothing to do with each other). It was also one of our best negotiations and helped grow our online sales. When we purchased Detroit-based American Blinds & Wallpaper Factory, we dubbed it Operation Century, because it had the potential to get us to $100 million in sales, which was a target for us. It was also something of a nostalgic coming full circle as one of my original inspirations for NoBrainerBlinds.com came from American Blinds. Looking at their sales model back in the '90s, I thought if you could sell blinds over the phone and by catalog, maybe you could sell them online.

American Blinds had been a mail order company with a significant portion of their sales in wallpaper, which had decreased in demand by about 80 percent over a ten-year period. So, not only was their business decreasing substantially, but their business model was antiquated. Catalogs were expensive to produce, to update, to mail, to buy address lists for, and American Blinds never evolved beyond them. In fact, when we spoke to them about merging, they had revenue of about $55 million. They suggested a 60-40 split, where they would own 60 percent of the combined company and we would get no cash. It didn't take a lot of consideration to see that this wasn't a good deal, as they were diminishing in stature, decreasing in volume, and had virtually no profit.

So, we waited.

We believed that they were heading for bankruptcy and fast—and that they were in a condition that no one could turn around unless they were already in the business. We'd already had the experience of buying BlindsWholesale in 2001 and JustBlinds in 2005, so we knew how to successfully buy and integrate companies. With American Blinds, we were essentially buying a customer list and more than fifty years of customer satisfaction.

However, despite their precarious position, the existing American Blinds management was arrogant. They overvalued themselves and did not believe they needed to change anything about how they did business. Watching this happen, it was hard to understand what they thought they were holding on to. The founder had already been pushed out when a private equity firm came in, but even that was tanking. This new PE fund had put a lot of money into the company, and soon we learned they were about to fold it up. Bingo. It was the perfect time for us to come in, and we bought them at a fire sale price. It was very difficult structurally, because of their debt and all the entities involved, but you couldn't beat the price—so low, we didn't even have to borrow money.

American Blinds' success selling blinds via mail order helped reinforce my initial kernel idea that online sales could work. Ironically, their leaders' own resistance to it also reinforced for me the need to **Evolve Continuously**, that first of the 4 core values. Their corporate arrogance prevented them from seeing their impending doom and taking any action to curb it. It prevented them several times from making ego-checking decisions that could have saved their company and helped their associates. It was clear when we entered their offices in Detroit for the first time that their people did not come first in their culture. I probably could have guessed that from their CEO's behavior.

The Detroit office was cavernous, dark, depressing. This once formidable organization that had employed hundreds of customer service representatives now had maybe seventy. We offered many of them jobs. The jobs required a move to Houston, which we thought might be appealing given how much stronger Houston's economy was than Detroit's at the time. However, only two took us up on the offer, including their head of HR, Kevin Barrios, who became our first HR director. Getting Kevin out of the American Blinds deal was an unexpected bonus.

American Blinds not only gave us our first HR director, but in some ways brought us our first CFO, Houston Lane, whom we hired as a consultant for the integration two months ahead of the purchase. Many companies use their existing team during an acquisition and then try to fit the new company and its people in. They make the purchase, and wait until afterward to figure out the strategy and execution plan. I get that the sale is the thing, but if you can figure out integration before a purchase, you can truly leverage what you're buying while ensuring a smooth path for your existing business and staff. Because of Houston's leadership and his comprehensive merger and acquisition experience, as well as strong sequencing skills, we had a road map ready to go on Day One. We knew exactly what we were going to do from the moment we closed.

He did such a good job that a couple of years later, we hired him as full-time CFO, a position we'd never filled before. Actually, we did not have a CFO *or* an HR director for the first fourteen years of our existence, even with sales in excess of $50 million. In retrospect, I had never realized how much value both could bring.

Houston also brought us two interesting mementos of our acquisition: the clock that hung in the American Blinds office, stopped precisely at the time the deal closed, and their movie theater–grade popcorn machine. That was us **Enjoying the Ride** in a macabre sort of way.

Looking back on that time, Houston recalled, "I started in early February, and the transaction closed on April 7. We did a little over two months of planning for the integration, and then we executed the integration over the following three months.

"There was a lot that needed to be done, and I think Jay recognized that if his team was responsible for managing all of those details, they would be distracted from their day jobs."

We needed to hire fifty people in Houston to accommodate the increased business, and we had to release seventy in Detroit. We contracted with Burnett Temporary Services in Houston to help us recruit and screen people. We shipped two truckloads' worth of equipment and assets down from Michigan. We auctioned off cubicles, computer equipment, a generator, and other unneeded equipment from the American Blinds office.

We minded that gap successfully, but even when companies do hire someone to help with integration, many do it wrong.

"The leaders of the project don't begin planning the integration until they know for certain the deal is going to happen," noted Houston. "Generally, that is about seven to ten days before it closes, which is way too late to begin planning."

When planning does begin, many leaders also don't involve the leadership of the acquired party, which is a mistake, as well. After I hired Houston, we had weekly meetings to discuss what needed to be done, to coordinate the effort and to gauge our readiness. Even before closing the deal, we invited members of the American Blinds leadership team to join those meetings so they could help us with the planning, which was critical.

For instance, it was in one of those meetings that their IT director noted a massive issue to which we were oblivious: due to their many catalogs, American Blinds had accumulated over nine hundred toll-free numbers that needed to be managed in some way.

"We hadn't thought to ask that in our due diligence," Houston said. "That never even occurred to us. So, inviting them early on, even before closing, gave us an opportunity to identify issues and begin thinking through them.

"It showed their leaders respect that we wanted their advice on how to combine these two businesses, as opposed to just coming in and telling them what they should do."

If we had acted like jerks, then the acquisition wouldn't have been nearly so smooth and successful. In Houston's recount, there were three things we did right that helped our acquisition succeed when so many fail:

3 TIPS FOR A SUCCESSFUL ACQUISITION INTEGRATION

1. Start well in advance.
2. Add bandwidth to your leadership team.
3. Respect the leaders of the target company.

Because of our execution strategy, right before the acquisition closed, we had our largest training class to date, with close to thirty people. We trained them so they'd be ready on the phones the minute the acquisition went live. Ahead of closing, we integrated the American Blinds catalog onto our platform, including the wallpaper. We were prepared for action, and it worked out great.

After the acquisition, a long-term decision we had to make was whether to actually sell wallpaper or not. Everyone on the team felt we should not—everyone except me. It was too different from what we were already doing, they said. And, someone else added, the Autobahn technology platform was a configuration engine to put different constraints, options, and permutations of near unlimited sizes together. It was not meant to sell a simple product (i.e., SKU), a ready-made blind, or a roll of wallpaper.

Additional pushback cited that wallpaper didn't fit well with our sales operations. The size of a wallpaper sale relative to a blind sale was extremely low, around an average ticket of $75 versus $350 for a blind sale. Wallpaper sales usually took longer, too, and because our sales team was paid partly on how much revenue they brought in, among other qualitative metrics, it didn't make sense for them or for the company to spend time on wallpaper.

But I was focused on our long-term vision and our long-term strategy. For me, the argument wasn't about whether wallpaper would be a profitable product for us in the short term. It was critical we demonstrated that we were not a one-trick pony—that we could sell more than blinds. So, as with the building of Autobahn, I overrode the team and made the decision that we would take on wallpaper and adapt our engine to sell it.

Although your team may be unified in understanding the importance of your end goal, there will be times when you, as the leader, must stand alone and stand strong to make reaching it possible. You are your company's best visionary, so when you find yourself disagreeing with your leadership team, ask yourself if they are focused on a different horizon. Are they looking short term while you have your sights set long term? As Margaret Thatcher said, "Consensus is the negation of leadership." Of course, you could also be wrong.

In the end, American Blinds did help us reach our goal revenue of $100 million. In fact, we reached $115 million, and it closed a couple of gaps, too, by bringing us our first CFO and HR director. The purchase of American Blinds helped demonstrate what I always knew: we had always been far more than a blinds company. And we got all of that for an amazing price.

PERSPECTIVES ON GROWTH

1. Start small and stay under the radar until your product or service is worth promoting. Great advertising will put a business not ready for prime time out of business due to bad word of mouth, or from not having the infrastructure to support the demand. What an unfortunate waste.
2. Building a business one customer at a time works at first, but you'll never build anything of substance without leveraging your strengths. Discover what you can do to either piggyback off others' existing success or create a platform where it's effortless to serve customers with as few people as possible.
3. Expect competitors and suppliers to try to thwart your success. Many will copy what you're doing, which frustrated many of my employees. However, view these things as a sign of success, and keep evolving faster than anyone else.

Things were looking up for GCC, but business is never smooth sailing for long. Despite our increased size, now we had a new obstacle: a fuzzy view of our future.

Fuzzy Wuzzy Was a Where

To have a shared vision, you must also have a shared past. I believe firmly in giving every new associate strong ties to our history and our journey. If they are going to be part of the future, they must understand where we came from. That's why artifacts from our company's past play heavily into our office design, including street signs with the names of people from over the years, meeting rooms named after key events and our core values, and more. This gives everyone the same foundation for the future.

It's not just new ideas that require your clear and compelling vision, but anything that involves significant change. Imagine how our top salesperson of all time, Dixie Dalton, might have felt upon hearing we were diverging from our highly profitable sole focus to launch our Measure & Install (M&I) program in 2018, which took us away from our core offering—do-it-yourself blinds—and back into people's homes, measuring and installing as in the Laura's days. At first, she might have thought it was going backward—that it was crazy. But this turned out to be the business model that has made her more successful than she ever dreamed.

She already thought my original idea—the one that earned her more than $1 million over twelve years—was nuts. "I would never fathom that we could have this successful business with people doing all the work themselves," Dixie said. "Everyone told him there was no way in the world he could sell a complex product to the public. But he said, 'I'm going to do it. And I'm going to make **Experiment Without Fear of Failure** my core mission statement.'"

Because Dixie trusted me in the early days and I had never given her reason not to, she gave me the benefit of the doubt and supported the new M&I program. I've said already that trust is a prerequisite for sharing a vision—stakeholders must be willing to hear you, and that means your reputation must be rock solid. I had the track record with Dixie to earn me that trust.

"And now look where we are," Dixie said proudly. "To me, if you can sell complex window blinds online with people measuring their own stuff, you can do that with anything. We've now tapped into the people who don't want to measure themselves, so we have the best of both worlds."

A Clear Vision No One Could See

Thinking big allowed me to create the concept of GCC—a platform to sell any hard-to-buy, configurable custom product online. But honing in on the ability to share that vision is what made it a reality. I shared the idea with Daniel after returning from that formative Alaskan cruise with my kids, early in our company's history.

"It was like he had an epiphany on the cruise," Daniel said, looking back. "This was the first trip he'd taken since his wife passed away, and he came back with this idea of being the best at selling custom products. A much broader vision than we had before. The idea of becoming much more than a blinds retailer was very motivational, even though, practically speaking, we didn't realize it for ten years.

"But it was a driving factor in why we were acquired," Daniel noted. "And why we got interesting developers and better-quality talent. I learned a ton about the idea of painting a vision. I once had a coach who told me the difference between where you are in the company, if you're a manager or director or vice president, is how broad your vision is. Are you looking one year away, three years, five years?

"It generally makes me uncomfortable to talk too much about something that is not going to come to fruition for a while, maybe because I'm afraid of letting people down. But it didn't make Jay uncomfortable to do that."

Daniel made it sound easy for me to paint a vision, but the reality requires conscious effort and a leap of faith. This isn't something I've done once. It wasn't just one magic Alaskan cruise that set things in motion, but it did provide me the opportunity to tap into resources

I already had and show me how to make seeing these visions a practice going forward. In 2015, just after our merger with The Home Depot (something I'll fully get into later in the book), I wanted to illustrate to our 175 associates, many of whom likely were very concerned about their futures, exactly what this partnership could do for the business they had worked so hard to grow.

I created what was called The 2020 Vision. It was a vision of who we were going to be as a result of Home Depot's power: The Home Depot's Center of Excellence for Configurable Products. My vision was conceptual, and wasn't suited to just words and storytelling. Since most people aren't conceptual, they have to physically see it to really understand. So, we created a brochure set five years ahead in the year 2020, illustrating who GCC was as if the vision had already happened. We divided the vision into critical topics for our business, including culture, products, service, what our facility looked like, and more.

We crafted several questions for each of these topics and spent one hour with each department over a couple of days. I explained to everyone what we were doing and gave each department a category and questions to answer. It's critical to have that trust and buy-in from your team, but also to include them in developing the vision. They know your business just as well as you do. Use *their* passion and knowledge to grow your vision.

After I'd made the rounds to each department, I took what we'd talked about to one of our graphic designers, who created a graphic brochure, including a rendering of what our campus would look like. In one week, we created a physical brochure and had it ready to present to the new Home Depot CEO, Craig Menear, who had just two months earlier taken over for Frank Blake, the CEO at the time of our merger.

The vision wasn't just about impressing our new boss. Over the next five years, we talked about it every day. We handed out more brochures, had meetings about it, included it in our weekly all-hands meetings, called SayJays (more on those later, too), and extolled our excitement to prospective associates. It was something Steve O'Connor, my then-CFO and eventual successor as GCC's president in May 2020, noticed right away.

"When I first started here," Steve said, "The 2020 Vision was on the walls, and he handed me the brochure. You start thinking, if we could do that, it would be amazing. You get focused on, I have to work not forty hours but eighty hours, not because I'm being forced to, but because I want to get there. Then you get a team of people who start igniting."

Igniting a team around a big idea takes time and repetition. And more repetition. And more.

"When he used to lead SayJays, I noticed he kept saying the same things over and over. But he would say them differently, because he's trying to get the message to stick," Steve remembered. "And he told me, 'It's incredibly important. Because if they hear once, they'll forget it. They need to hear it this way; they need to hear it that way.' He'll definitely steer the message—he'll influence. He's not a directive decision maker. He's more about building consensus."

People need to be clear about where they're headed and how their trajectory aligns with that of the whole. If you tell somebody, "Here's where you are, here's what you do, here's where we're going, and this is why what you're doing is important," they're much more bought in to the company as a unit. And they do a much better job.

A leader who is more clearly aligned on operations, efficiency, and execution gets the right people. With this in mind, we began discussing The 2020 Vision in job interviews, because if you're doing something lofty and ambitious, you need people who think loftily and ambitiously. It was tremendous for hiring. It brought us Seth Todd, whom you'll remember I recruited *away* from Home Depot to become our Chief Digital Officer.

"When I met Jay, our first conversation was about these long-term things," Seth said about his coming aboard. "What can the company do? What can I do with the power of Home Depot? What can we do with the technology? What is your vision of where this goes long term? And in that conversation, I was able to be honest and say, 'This is what I see long term and what I want to do,' which aligned with his long-term vision."

6 STEPS FOR CREATING A TANTALIZING AND EFFECTIVE VISION TO POWER GROWTH

1. Be extremely clear. No vagueness.
2. Words matter, so use inspiring ones, like Vision 2020.
3. Repeat it. Repeat it again. Once more. Another time just to be sure.
4. Add graphics—make it visual.
5. Generate ownership of the idea by including your team in growing it.
6. Talk about it constantly. In every department and every critical step of your company.

I convinced Seth, who had managed thousands of people in Atlanta with Home Depot, that it was a good move for him to join us and take over a staff of forty. Later, I asked him to trust me one more time and help create a new division, our version of R&D, that would operate as autonomously as possible from GCC and Home Depot. He could have near complete control, but only three associates. Three people, yes, but those three people were steering a rocket.

An effective leader must be able to both paint a long-term vision and take dead aim on today's tasks. Prioritize your to-do list and narrow it down to a ninety-day plan. From that, create your team's swim lanes. For example, this is what Marketing is going to do, this is what Accounting is going to do, and this is what we need to work on together. With each team doing their part, a company can work on goals together as one larger team.

MIND THE GAPS

Readying Yourself and Your Team for the Inevitable Disruptions and Stress

Beginners get excited when they know the answer.
Masters get excited when they don't.

—Joel Marsh

One of the most critical leadership mandates is to mind the gaps. And there are always gaps. You close one, another appears. We bought American Blinds, but were left with the gap of how to integrate such a complicated and old-fashioned company without overloading ourselves and our team. Your job as a leader is not to eradicate gaps, but rather to be aware of them and how they affect your people and your business. Predict them, mind them, and bridge them when it makes sense. Then begin again.

Growth inevitably creates more and more gaps. Some gaps you can live with longer than others. You must be able to predict how long you can live with a gap before it begins to erode what you've built.

For instance, when we were growing rapidly for five or six years straight in the early 2010s, I knew our biggest gap was talent management and development. I saw the locomotive bearing down on us and knew we were going to get to the point where people were in positions that had outgrown them and I wasn't able to train them anymore. It would severely damage our company to ignore that gap, so we created the position of Chief People Officer. This role was tasked with creating an organizational structure and professional development path. That structure eventually became the ILIAD, GCC's talent development and learning center, which will be more fully explained in a later chapter.

In short: as a leader, you must be able to see the gaps in your company and fill them quickly.

Know When You're the Pig

It's not just about bridging gaps in your organization, strategy, tactics, products, services, or people. It's also, and maybe especially, about minding your own personal gaps. If you put lipstick on a pig, it's still a pig. Know when you're the pig.

Often, these are the most difficult gaps to see, but trust me, you have gaps. We all do. And the sooner and more accurately you identify them, the faster you can mitigate them. One of my gaps used to be (and still is to some extent, I suppose) the way I gave people news I knew they didn't want to hear, such as, "No, you are not getting the role you expected."

Always looking out for my employees' well-being, I'd sugarcoat the information to the point where people did not know what I was trying to convey, which ended up being worse than just being direct, despite my best intentions. I received that feedback not only from my associates, but from my kids. "Dad, just say it!" was a common refrain in our house. What's particularly mystifying to me is that I've always told people to be candid with me, but I was often not being candid with others. One of my and my company's core values is **Express Yourself**, and yet it was many years until I finally began to be more forthright.

I was the pig, too, when I would coach associates on their sales skills *while* they were on the phone with a customer. At the time, it seemed so reasonable, but later, Ann told me she used to cry when I did that. In hindsight, what I did sounds ridiculous to me. Oink!

Sometimes you bridge your gaps through personal development and learning. Mostly you do it by hiring those with skill sets that both complement and greatly exceed your own.

You need to do both. Often.

If you've heard of just-in-time manufacturing, I'm a just-in-time learner. I focus on what I need to know now, or will need to know soon, and fill that gap. For instance, when I needed to know about branding and hiring and organizational design, I found the best books and articles on those topics and read them. I identified the gap and closed it. As I've said before, my ignorance and lack of formal business training ultimately turned out to be a strength. I knew so little about how to do so many things that I had not had the chance to develop too many bad habits. When I *needed* to know something, I went and learned it, coming in fresh. Learning best practices was key to my success.

Instead of just talking about what these best practices were, or vaguely referencing that one *should* be reading and seeking them, let me give you a guide. The following books influenced me the most, but in different ways. In some cases, a single idea in a single line catalyzed a decision that proved highly impactful. Others I go back to time and time again for the whole package. No doubt there were scores, if not hundreds, of other books and articles that provided insight and valuable information, though I'm probably biased by the *availability factor*, where your brain has a tendency to judge matters by the first thing that comes to mind, as described in Daniel Kahneman's book, *Thinking Fast and Slow*.

The recency and frequency of information also has a tendency to bias your end-of-year annual performance reports whereby the last thing you remember about an associate taints the entire report, so be conscious of that. Moreover, the way your brain plays tricks on you is widely researched and written about (e.g., *Predictably Irrational* by Dan Ariely and *Stumbling on Happiness* by Daniel Gilbert), so I'll leave it to you to read those if the topic is of interest. Regardless of how you choose which book to read next, consider something other than the topic of business per se, and consider topics that will help you better understand people and the way they (and you) think. Oftentimes, these books are the biggest teachers.

Here are my book game changers:

- *Man's Search for Meaning* by Victor Frankl—Put life in perspective for me, providing equanimity.
- *The Happiness Hypothesis* by Jonathan Haidt—Helped me to understand key contributors of happiness and life satisfaction, with perspective on how your brain affects that.
- *Built to Last* by Jim Collins—First book to show how purpose foundationally affects success.

- *Good to Great* by Jim Collins—Inspired my BHAG (Big Hairy Audacious Goal) and mission—and was the genesis for my thirst for nonfiction reading.
- *Guerrilla Marketing* by Jay Conrad Levinson—Gave me the hope and optimism that I could market effectively with little money.
- *The Five Dysfunctions of a Team* by Patrick Lencioni—Full of ideas to conquer a leadership team's poor dynamics.
- *The Innovator's Dilemma* by Clayton Christensen—Gave me a better understanding of why the entrepreneur's mindset to disrupt is antithetical to many corporate executives.
- *Tell to Win* by Peter Guber—Taught me how to pitch ideas and effectively raise money.
- *You're Not the Person I Hired!* by Janet Boydell, Barry Deutsch, and Brad Remillard—A good discussion of how to hire objectively and ensure you're considering the right hiring criteria.
- *Positioning: The Battle for Your Mind* by Al Ries, Jack Trout, and Philip Kotler—Primer on anchoring and other key concepts.
- *The Discipline of Market Leaders* by Fred Wiersema and Michael Treacy—Aided my understanding of how GCC differed from Home Depot.
- *The 5 Love Languages* by Gary Chapman—The template for reconciling how GCC differed from Home Depot. Helped my marriage, too!
- *Getting to Yes: Negotiating Agreement Without Giving In* by Roger Fisher, William L. Ury, and Bruce Patton—Introduced me to the Best Alternative to a Negotiated Agreement (BATNA), which I've since applied to negotiations and all interactions, including meetings.

- *Blueprint to a Billion: 7 Essentials to Achieve Exponential Growth* by David G. Thomson—Inspired our white-label platforms with Sears and Wayfair, leading to enhanced valuation with acquirers and eventual merger.
- *Principles* by Ray Dalio—Where I learned about asynchronous risk, uncorrelated paths to a goal, and understanding errors in systems versus people.
- *Creativity, Inc.* by Ed Catmull and Amy Wallace—Improved and facilitated our post-merger relationship with Home Depot, helping to maximize value to both GCC and Home Depot.
- *Dual Transformation: How to Reposition Today's Business While Creating the Future* by Scott D. Anthony, Clark G. Gilbert, and Mark W. Johnson—A look at how to organize your company's structure to simultaneously pursue high growth *and* focus on the core.
- *High Output Management* by Andy Grove—A primer on organizational structure and process geared to scale a business with leverage, with lessons too numerous to mention.
- *Discovery-Driven Growth: A Breakthrough Process to Reduce Risk and Seize Opportunity* by Ian C. MacMillan and Rita Gunther McGrath—Insight on how to plan and execute projects with ambiguity and perspective on how those projects should fit into your overall initiative portfolio.

I've found that the associates of mine who read the most were usually those most eager to evolve and most willing to experiment. That resulted in their being most likely to grow their careers, get the opportunity to earn higher levels of responsibility, and make more money. The goal of reading is not just to learn a specific thing, but to prime your brain to readily accept new data from many sources, and to be attentive to converting that data into useful information to improve everything and everyone.

I've always encouraged reading among my staff and over time became more intentional about it. We started a monthly GCC book club, a great idea suggested by one of our associates. Outside of the book club, we discussed books that had been instrumental in sparking new initiatives and strategies, often buying copies for our senior leadership team to read. Finally, in 2013, we turned one of our small conference rooms into a library of books we'd read, available for anyone to pick off the shelves and return once finished. It was aptly named the GCC Library, complete with a quaint swinging sign just outside the door.

If you think you don't have time to read, remember that, as a leader, a big part of your job is to learn. It follows, then, that an express part of your job description is to read. Thus, reading is an integral component of your daily activities and not something for which you merely try to make time.

Feeling Like a Fraud

Moving from considering myself an idealistic entrepreneur to becoming a CEO managing a team of capable executives was a huge change for me, and one I wasn't prepared for. I was confident as the owner of my company, but sometime around 2005, just after buying JustBlinds, I realized I had no idea what I was supposed to do as a CEO. I felt like a fraud, which I later discovered is a common sensation (though that doesn't necessarily make it any easier to experience), and is referred to as "imposter syndrome."

Looking for guidance, I turned to the CEO peer support group Vistage. Fredricka (Fred) Brecht was my chair for eleven years. During those years, she and I met alone for two hours each month to work on my professional development, and then I spent a separate full day each month with the peer group, made up of about a dozen CEOs from different industries in Houston.

Fred was one of the first people to help me understand that my greatest value to the company was not in the tasks I could perform, but in helping others to their highest potential, in filling those gaps between current performance and potential capability. Leaders should be judged not so much by what they do, but by how well their people do.

"I think he really became an expert at inspired hiring," Fred said retrospectively, six years after I left Vistage. "He hired really capable people and spiraled them to a really impressive level of commitment, and in the course of doing that he leveraged himself. When he shifted to say, 'I have to accomplish everything through others,' it was such an accelerator."

Fred's right. When I left behind my value as a doer and embraced the value of my inherent belief in people, that's when our company truly took off. When someone brought me a problem, I resisted the urge to solve it for them. That is not my value. They know the problem and the circumstances around it better than anyone. It would be arrogant and ineffective for me to try to jump in and solve an issue that belongs to someone else. What they're really asking me for, and the value I can provide to them as a leader, is to coach them *through* the problem, to fill that gap of what they aren't yet seeing or don't yet understand.

I begin by asking them what their goal is and what they've already tried. Then I ask what they believe might work and why. This last question is crucial to learning how someone thinks and is a barometer for determining latitude in how you might delegate or promote them. It's also crucial that the employee trusts that I really am asking for all their ideas—and that no idea is a bad one. The core value **Express Yourself** doesn't work if people don't feel free to be honest. As a leader, you must lay that trust over and over through example.

Like many founders, I was afraid to take on the responsibility of delegation, but no matter how adept your hiring, you'll never fully leverage your people if you don't delegate. You must give them autonomy with clear expectations, but as I discussed in the section on building trust back in Chapter 3, you also don't completely abdicate until people have proven themselves. So, you delegate a little, then gradually more to those who satisfy your expectations. Your default goal is to delegate everything except the ultimate accountability for everything, which is a paradox (a topic more fully explained in Chapter 11). You may not get there fully, but that's your goal.

And if you hire well, it makes it a lot easier to delegate. Not only will you be more confident in the people to whom you're delegating, but they'll be eager to take on your work. That, by the way, doesn't mean you abdicate final responsibility. You are always responsible for all results. Leverage your people, allow them to develop skills and experience, and in the process your organization becomes more efficient. Putting your ego aside, there's not a whole lot that only you can do.

Heavy Is the Head

As a leader, you're often going to experience high levels of stress. How you manage that stress is critical not only to your own health, but to the health of your company. Using your stress is a critical leadership trait.

Running a company is fun, but many don't appreciate the incessant pressure, not just from your investors and your board, but the pressure you will put on yourself. You'll fret over many things, such as profit, gross margin, strategy, advertising, and other cognitive considerations.

BEFORE YOU GO INTO BUSINESS, CONSIDER HOW YOU MIGHT HANDLE THESE 10 GUT-WRENCHING STRESS-INDUCERS

1. Bringing home enough money (e.g., debt, personal guarantees)
2. Spending enough time at home with family and friends (i.e., work-life balance)
3. Dealing with the paranoia of ensuring that you remain relevant, learn fast enough, think far enough ahead, and evolve the company and yourself
4. Raising capital
5. Losing control through dilution (i.e., owning less of your company by selling some of it to others)
6. Being responsible for your associates' futures
7. Terminating associates and being unsure what to do about nonperformers
8. Learning to deal with your own emotional intelligence
9. Having the ability to make decisions with imperfect data (dealing with ambiguity)
10. Being able to calculate how much risk is too much risk

The only way you'll get through it is by consistent awareness. Leaders must practice constant threat vigilance, meaning you are acutely alert and responsive to the threats and opportunities around you—many of which you can only imagine. You must scan the horizon at all times, always looking a few steps ahead at how today's activities or sales will impact your decisions tomorrow.

However, this heightened awareness is not to be confused with the hypervigilance you might experience in extreme stress. When hypervigilance stress takes over, you become paranoid and are more likely to have knee-jerk reactions instead of thoughtful responses to challenges.

In times of heightened stress, like the months leading up to our merger with Home Depot, I learned not to combat the stress but to accept it. I never knew from where the next onslaught of threats might come— investors, board members, employees, attorneys. It was by being self-aware of threat vigilance that I stayed healthy and productive rather than overly sensitive and obsessive.

In general, I've always managed stress well, and that's been an asset. I find you must have perspective, or everything will seem like a four-alarm fire. I have a 1–10 scale for myself, where 10 is the best day ever, and 1 equals death. Most days, I'm between 3 and 8. Although that 3–8 range can be intense, it's good intensity, because I'm working on things I want to work on that are important. Figure out what a personal 10 means to you, a personal 1, and a personal 5, and begin to weigh everything around that metric.

One of the ways I manage my stress is to honor my routines. They may seem silly or small to others, but they are critical to me, and, thankfully, my wife, Barbara, understands that. In the morning, I prefer solitude and quiet so I can ease into the day. In this order, I (1) feed the dog, (2) listen to very quiet music (usually a playlist I've created of about three hundred pieces of light classical music), (3) take vitamins, (4) make coffee, (5) meditate (in a particular chair), (6) note three specific things for which I'm grateful, and (7) note the three most important things I intend to do that day. You get primed for the day, you're grateful, and have a road map. Ready! True to my commitment to always being open to learning and absorbing information from media in any form, when Tony Robbins mentioned his meditation regimen of gratitude and intent in an interview as being a morning ritual of his, it made a significant difference for me.

Then, it's time to get activated. Later in the morning, I'll read the news, check emails, and look at my to-do list so I know exactly what I'm going to accomplish every day. A to-do list is critical to maintaining my stress levels. It helps me be prepared and well organized. When you habitually follow a morning regimen, your mind is less filled with wondering what you should do, and instead you can just do what you already know to do, freeing up your mind for substance. It might sound counterintuitive, but in reality, structure creates opportunity for spontaneity.

At night, I don't read email or look at my phone for the hour before I go to bed, which helps me ease out of the day. I also won't engage in challenging conversations during that time.

Barbara explained, "Over the years, I've come to really appreciate Jay's discipline and that's one of his qualities that I admire. He works intensely, manages his time well, and knows when to stop."

I also work out three to four mornings a week, and if I feel myself being overtaken by stress during the workday, I retreat to my office, which has low lighting and noise filters, and shut the door. That gives me a chance to recharge. It does mean that when I go in to close off the world, it also closes off people from seeing me. I know that's an issue, but in moments like these, the greater issue is to first take care of myself so that I am able to take care of others.

My hobbies also help me manage stress. For me, hobbies are not about business. I don't hit the golf course to close a deal or join a country club for business development. My hobbies are an extension of my pursuit of **the 4 Es**: **Evolve**, **Experiment**, **Express**, and **Enjoy**. My life values match the core values of my company, which makes it easy to lead by example.

While hobbies are great for stress management, if you're a leader focused entirely on business, that's a big gap in your ability to relate to your people and others, as well as in your personal life. The freedom to pursue them along with your business comes only with the support of your family. In my case, this includes Barbara, to whom I am grateful. Even though I don't pursue hobbies for professional reasons, that isn't to say they don't help me with business. I have spent nearly fifty years singing with the same barbershop quartet, beginning in our days at the University of Texas at Austin. We call ourselves the 40 Acre 4 because UT's campus was originally built on forty acres. To be successful, we do extensive research and collaborate as a group to select our music. Then, we create a project plan of sorts to interpret the piece for each voice. We spend hours in rehearsal to ensure the final outcome is amazing. In retrospect, *amazing* only applies to our younger days singing. Certainly, there are lessons and skills there that are synonymous with running a company.

In my office at GCC rests a pair of boxing gloves signed by the associates of JustBlinds.com after we purchased the company. They wanted me to know they were fighting right alongside me—a generous and meaningful gift, especially because I have boxed for almost twenty years. When I look back on my hundreds of hours in the boxing gym, I realize the sport has taught me much about patience, stamina, and intuition, which are critical qualities for a leader.

Hours and hours of boxing fundamentals drills ingrains them in you, leaving your brain open to outthink your opponent in a match. This is not dissimilar to the intense training new employees receive, drilling product and service basics into them, allowing their brains to be ready to solve customer challenges.

Before I started boxing, I didn't know how well I could push myself through pain and exhaustion. There's something that happens in your brain when you're in the tenth round with two minutes to go in a 110-degree gym—and that mental stamina sticks around outside the ring.

If your hobbies make you a better leader, great. If they make you a better, happier human, terrific. The key is they should fit your core values so they accentuate who you are and help you be better than you ever dreamed possible.

Here's a trick. If you're not sure what your core values are, inspect your hobbies and where you spend the most time. I'll bet you'll see what it is about them that propels you.

Delegate, Dummy

When I hired Larry, it was easy to delegate technology to him because I knew nothing about it and he was the clear expert. Then I brought in Daniel, because I needed somebody analytical who could develop our marketing. With Larry, Daniel, and Steve Riddell on my team, I saw the value of delegation a lot better because they could all do things I could never do as well.

But, again, you must start with the right raw materials. You can't delegate to just anyone. Hiring exceptional people is what lets you focus farther down the horizon and grow your business exponentially. While my executive coaching style is to open things up, my interview method is to drill down as narrowly as possible with the candidate. Perhaps more than the actual questions I ask, it's that relentless prodding that reveals whether the applicant will be a fit.

For example, if I ask, "What do you think about continuous improvement?" I may get a vague answer, such as, "I very much believe in continuous improvement. I think it's very important."

My next question would be, "What are you doing currently to improve yourself?" And if the answer remains vague or if there's any opportunity to drill deeper, I ask another follow-up, and another. This is the single best interview technique I know for detecting bullshit.

And while I'm conducting an interview, I seldom show any facial expressions, which, I've been told, can be downright upsetting to the other party. In fact, and I'm not proud of this, several individuals have cried during interviews with me. It became common enough that my team created a saying for the occurrence: "Jayed," as in, "That person was Jayed."

Unfortunately, the term also included more casual conversations I had with associates, when my curiosity and direct style of questioning simply got the better of me.

I believe strongly in management by walking around. Get up and see what's going on. Leave your office. Following that model, I often engaged in casual conversations with my team. I asked what they were working on, what was getting in their way, things like that. Apparently, the fact that I was truly interested and began drilling down with more questions, rather than letting the conversations end casually, surprised and unsettled some associates.

Unprepared to be deeply questioned by the CEO, associates might feel stumped and say something, anything, even if they were guessing and knew it might not be true. And then I would follow up on it. And then they would feel really bad. But I wasn't doing that on purpose to put people on the spot. I genuinely cared and wanted to help.

One of the questions I often asked was, "Is there anything I can do to help you with your job? Or is there anything we can do to make it easier for you?" Those are critical questions to ask, and, while my style in asking may have been less than graceful, asking people when they haven't had time to think about the potential consequences of an answer yields more honest responses. And, as a leader, that's the most valuable thing your team can give you: honesty.

Being deliberate about encouraging others to express themselves, whether it be about an initiative or inclusivity, for example, cannot be stressed enough; however, as much as you reinforce and even implore people to do so, it is still your responsibility to seek the truth.

5 ESSENTIAL WAYS TO ENSURE YOU GET THE TRUTH

1. Randomly attend department meetings. Watch if others are speaking up and how the leaders are responding, and whether they are developing their direct reports.
2. Receive reports at a consistent cadence and ensure you read them knowing that both you and the preparer might have confirmation bias, which could skew the conclusions.
3. Hold one-to-one meetings, not so much to review progress on initiatives, but instead to understand what might be getting in their way.
4. Keep your organization as flat as possible. Hierarchy and bureaucracy are the death knell of companies.
5. Set the example by always telling the truth, so others will feel free to be candid.

It's also the most valuable thing you can give your associates. It's why the question I suggest asking job candidates about what they're doing to improve themselves is critical.

Accepting feedback is a key part of continuous improvement. Hearing from others will end up being about 25 percent of your self-improvement. But the preponderance must come inwardly. Being able to assess your own areas of improvement is critical to your growth, so it's helpful to deduce a candidate's self-awareness, honesty, and lack of ego. An effective way to do this is to end each interview with this question: "How well do you think you did in this interview?"

Our culture is so critical to our success that we interview substantially for it. Our number one objective is to find someone who is not just comfortable with, but excited by, an environment where we expect them to evolve daily—not someone who staunchly insists on stability. If someone demonstrates that they already do that in their personal lives, they'll thrive at GCC.

"If you ask my team, I think most would say that's their favorite core value," Seth said of **Evolve Continuously**. "If you're not a person who wants to do that, you're probably not going to fit in great. I try to push that as hard as I can with my people. You have to challenge yourself all the time. If you're not getting better, you're probably getting worse."

I reiterated that expectation immediately by speaking to every new hire class for an hour on our core values. When we got to **Experiment Without Fear** and **Evolve Continuously**, I first asked them, "What do you think that means?" And we talked about what the expectations were.

I told them very clearly, "If you don't evolve, you're not going to keep up and you're not going to be here. To not evolve is a job-threatening decision. But if you do evolve, you will get ahead. You also need to help the people around you evolve, you need to help your team evolve, and your team needs to help other teams evolve. Then we need to help our vendors, investors—all stakeholders. Ultimately, focusing on helping everyone means you'll always be focused on your customers."

We have a large whiteboard called the Evolve Continuously Board, where associates publicly announce things they're doing to improve themselves, usually having nothing to do with the business, such as losing weight, training for a marathon, being more patient with their kids, taking cooking lessons, and so forth. It helps to make a proclamation so others can help keep you accountable. This also reinforces that we wanted to help people become better at everything in their lives, not just improve for the business's sake. The idea occurred to me when I visited Zappos's office and saw a small whiteboard hanging outside a counselor's office, where people posted topics they felt the company needed to address.

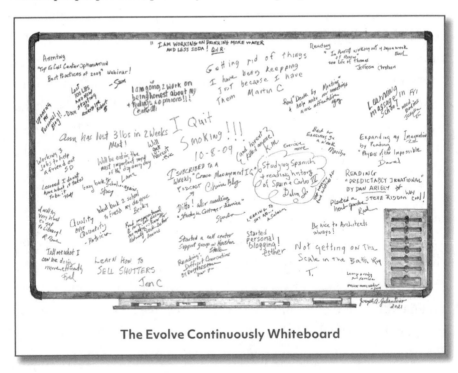

The Evolve Continuously Whiteboard

The ability to evolve continuously means someone is adaptable, which means they are less likely to be afraid of change, which is business's only constant. That was something Larry looked for when he was building his technology team.

"Things change all the time. We want people who can adapt and do different things. I loved it when I first joined the company, because I got to do a very eclectic [mix] of things. As the CIO, I might be planning the budget for next year; I might be doing strategic planning with the leadership team; or I might be in one of the conference rooms, installing a screen and a projector from the ceiling and running cabling and then writing some code," Larry noted.

Larry's zest for life, diversification, and his ability to recruit and build amazing teams were noticed particularly when Home Depot did their due diligence several years later. Sami Nassar, one of the two people assigned to lead the diligence, told me six years after the merger that at the time he'd wondered, "Is Larry that good, or does the team just love him?"

In my view, Larry was admired for a couple of reasons. He was a "players' coach"—he had done the work his team was doing and maintained his love of coding. He was able to recruit top talent who didn't just possess high standards but were also disruptive and wanted to make a difference. These are important attributes for a growing business.

Larry gave his direct reports a lot of latitude, too, allowing people to make mistakes, even when he could see those mistakes coming. We disagreed about how much latitude to give. I was a bit more cautious, but I trusted Larry. His enthusiasm extended to life in general, too. Apparently, after a Home Depot technology analyst spent most of a day with Larry, Larry told him, "There are three things I'm passionate about: coding, cave diving, and sex." As I said—diversification.

Please Be So Kind as to Leave Now

Because our culture is radically nonhierarchical, candidates who are driven by true success and not the commonly accepted indicators of it, such as a corner office, will excel. Conversely, those who do value titles and emblems of power will quickly feel uncomfortable in our office, which thrives on collaboration, transparency, and accidental interactions.

Larry also watched for this in interviews: "You had to find people who were entrepreneurial, who liked our environment and wanted to do lots of different things. So, if people were too preoccupied with the space or seemed put off by it, it was a red flag, because that's not the priority. Our priority is building something that's going to be really cool."

Entrepreneurial people are faster to embrace, and usually already have in their lives, the core value of **Experiment Without Fear of Failure**. That's why my second go-to interview question is: "Give me some examples of things you've done that took courage or a time you did something you've never done before." If, for example, they say they once grabbed $50 and a friend and went backpacking across Vietnam on a whim, that might indicate a lack of planning to another hiring manager, but to me, it would be a fantastic answer.

Because we encourage entrepreneurialism and our goal is to help people become better than they ever believed possible, that sometimes means helping them ultimately leave the company. Many of my leaders had entrepreneurial ambitions of their own, which is what makes them such effective leaders. While it may feel counterintuitive, encourage your associates to be open and honest about their personal goals and to **Express Themselves**, and make it everyone's responsibility to help them achieve those goals.

Seth believes this type of transparency results in better hiring and productivity. "I'd much rather things be clear, with open expectations, and find out how we mutually get everybody what they want out of the situation," he said. "When I interview, I ask, 'How long do you want to be here? What do you want to do?' And if, five years from now, you want to be an underwater basket weaver, if you spend two years here or even if you spend twelve months here, and you create value for me, I'll do everything I can to make you an underwater basket weaver. And we'll both walk away happy, and everything will be great.

"If I don't know that, and you leave thirteen months from now, and I don't even know why and I wasn't ready for it, that's worse. If you know what motivates everybody, if you know why everybody's here, you know what they want to be here for. We're here to make people better than they ever thought possible. If we make that a real thing for people, they work harder. If I can help them do whatever it is that they want to do two years from now, they'll work nights, evenings, weekends, they'll work twice as hard here as they will if they're focused all that time on figuring out what it is they want to be doing two years from now."

While there are many examples of people staying longer than they intended because they enjoyed working at GCC, Seth draws an important point about that: "If everybody stays because we make it so great, then I'm probably somewhere in there commuting the process. I'm not really helping them get to what they want to do. But for every one of those people who leaves here and feels like they left here able to do what they want to do because we helped them do it, I probably get two to four referrals, and I get somebody else in here who's coming for the right reason."

I feel great pride for the entrepreneurs who have found their voices inside the walls of GCC. One of my greatest joys in that area is Esther, my oldest child, who joined us right after graduating from college, doing administrative work in the Marketing department for Daniel.

"By the end of it, I was doing all the PR and social media," Esther said.

It was Esther who first told me about Twitter, which had questionable value then. Since I believe strongly that to learn something you need to actually do it, I decided to open an account and get busy. I was so active that I was included on a list of the most popular CEOs on social media, ranked one slot ahead of Donald Trump. Not anymore.

"It was a very rewarding experience," Esther said of her time at GCC. "It was really hard and really fast-paced. I was recruited all the time, but there wasn't another place in Houston that offered me as good of an experience and was so forward-thinking. There was nowhere better for me to be."

Esther left the company in 2012 when she started her own business, Cuteheads.com, where she designs and sells unique children's clothing online. That business is now more than a decade old, which is an incredible accomplishment in the e-commerce world.

"I still use a lot of the skills I learned [at GCC], the processes and the organization tools—things I never would have learned in college," she said.

Running her own business also allows Esther, now Esther Freedman, to be a full-time mom to her two daughters, Naomi (named after my first wife) and Tova, and son, Micah.

The goal is not to keep employees forever. The goal is to help them become better than they ever dreamed possible. But while they are with us, the combination of hundreds of people sharing our four core values creates a ride-or-die passion for GCC. We are a tribe of individuals who have in common a mission and the means by which we execute it.

Nothing Exposes Gaps like a Crisis

During hard times—and every business faces hard times that often can't be predicted, such as natural disasters or pandemic viruses—your gaps will become much wider and more difficult to bridge. Do as much as you can to close them before an emergency is at hand. It's too hard to change tires while you're driving the car.

Make sure you have a solid business continuity plan that's been tested and tweaked. And continue tweaking it during the crisis, and afterward. During a crisis, you need constant communication, including multiple, planned daily check-ins with your team. If you already do a weekly meeting, keep it. Find a way to use technology to not only keep up your communication, but to amplify it.

During a crisis is when your core values are especially important. Your values, whatever they are, should be your North Star, guiding your actions when decisions need to be decisive, despite ambiguous or uncertain times. Never be uncertain of your core values. Make them part of your constant conversations with associates. Remind them what you and your organization stand for. That consistency is comforting during unsettling times.

"Our core values were kind of intended for a time like this," Omair Tariq, COO of GCC until 2020, told our team during the first remote Say-Jay broadcast after the first week of stay-at-home orders due to the 2020 COVID-19 global pandemic, when much of our team was working from home. "We are evolving continuously as this situation changes. We are experimenting with new tools and technology. We are expressing ourselves, speaking up when things are working well and when things are not. Most important, we are enjoying the ride."

It's important during stressful and uncertain times to maintain a sense of humor and lightheartedness. Let your team know it's OK to bring levity to a tough situation. For instance, three weeks into the pandemic, when everyone was working from home, during our second virtual Say-Jay, the Marketing department joked about what a challenge working from home was for so many of us. Members of the team pretended to share serious updates while wrangling unruly kids or upset pets. They clearly were trying to **Enjoy the Ride**, even when the ride was bumpy.

A crisis highlights existing gaps, and it gives you the opportunity to evolve not only continuously, but quickly. Innovation often is the result of solving a difficult challenge with limited resources.

9 WAYS TO READY YOUR TEAM FOR AN AMBIGUOUS AND ROCKY FUTURE

1. Admit early on that you don't know exactly what you're doing, because vulnerability will give others the chance to feel your compassion for what they're feeling. And remember, they know less about the future than you do.
2. Acknowledge that it will be hard, preparing them so that when they feel the pain, it won't be such a surprise.
3. Be clear about where you're going, but also that it's acceptable not to know exactly how you're going to get there.
4. Frequently and passionately stress the vison so everyone knows why you're all *suffering*.
5. Recruit only those people who relish ambiguity. Believe me, that whittles down your choices.
6. Openly seek and be open to feedback.
7. Understand that each person accepts change at a different pace, so your communication might be accepted by some but others might need a different approach, or more time.
8. Focus on the most difficult problems first so that you don't pick off the easy stuff only to find out later that the most daunting obstacle thwarts you, thereby causing you to spend time and money needlessly. Human nature causes most to do the easy things first.
9. Celebrate success and provide public recognition often.

This is also the time when your culture of generosity takes over. Your leadership must exhibit empathetic behavior, irrespective of rules and regulations. For instance, in March 2020, during the COVID-19 crisis, if someone couldn't work from home, we gave them the opportunity to work in the office as long as no one else was close by. Ultimately, conditions mandated that no one be in the office, but business was still thriving as customers stuck in their houses revved up home improvement projects. During COVID-19 and the multiple hurricanes we had in prior years weathered in Houston, for those associates without adequate transportation or with kids at home, we brought them the tools and equipment they needed to do their jobs.

When generosity comes from the top, it becomes part of your company's culture. It permeates walls and offices and cubicles and becomes the expected and underlying tone of every interaction between associates and consequently between your associates and your customers.

"Our biggest accomplishment really is Hurricane Harvey," said Shannon Campbell, my executive assistant, who has been with GCC more than a decade. "We had twenty or thirty people flooded out of their homes, including myself. We found hotel rooms for them to stay in. We rented cars for people. Home Depot was amazing—they helped us secure rooms and cars.

"The company came together. There were people who lost their homes, and their entire department helped them rip out their waterlogged walls and floors. How we responded to that and helped people out really touched a lot of people and made a difference in their lives."

Another quality that helps teams through a crisis is grit, which I believe could be the single biggest driver of effective leadership and execution. Grit most often comes from surviving adversity. It's certainly something I valued in my team. Our grit was first tested during Hurricane Ike in 2008. Larry had joined the company just a year before.

"We lost power for a week," he remembered. "One of the guys on the IT team was able to secure a generator, but it only held enough gas to run until about 3:00 a.m. So, he would come out around 2:30 a.m. with gas. The generator was running in the parking lot, and we ran an extension cord all the way from there, through the hallway, up the stairs, and into the server room, so we could plug in the servers and keep them running. At that time we were hosting our own servers, and it became abundantly obvious we needed to stop doing that.

"Even though nobody was working in that facility, we were still running the website from this generator. And that was the work ethic we expected from people. You did whatever it took to keep things working. You did whatever was in your job description, plus anything else that needed to be done."

If you're lucky enough to survive long enough, your company will be rocked by multiple crises. Prepare for them by minding your gaps, having a tested business continuity plan, and ensuring that generosity and grit are woven heavily into your culture.

ONE THING. JUST ONE THING
Crafting the Right Culture

*If you get the culture right, most of the other
stuff will just take care of itself.*

—Tony Hsieh

The comedy film *City Slickers* is one of my favorites, about people vacationing at a dude ranch searching for their existential purpose. The head cowboy, Curly, played by actor Jack Palance, tells Billy Crystal's character, Mitch, "One thing. Just one thing. You stick to that and the rest don't mean shit." Curly died before Mitch learned what Curly meant. But in business, I think I know the one thing: culture.

Global Custom Commerce has many times been recognized as The Best Place to Work in Houston, among the elite in Texas, and honored with several national awards of employee engagement. We're pleased to have won them in each size category as we grew our associate count over the years. In virtually every case, they acknowledged the unique culture we enjoy.

That culture was created diligently and intentionally. I strove through my words, actions, and demeanor to convey our culture to anyone we came into contact with, or who came into contact with us. That's still evident in every fiber of our office—literally.

The selection and placement of every square of carpeting and piece of furniture in the office were approved with care and mindfulness—by me. I was intricately involved in laying out and designing every step of our ninety-thousand-square-foot office. I named every one of the many conference rooms to honor our company's history, so we ended up with the Van, honoring my original means of transporting blinds to customers, the Garage, where it all started in my home, and many others.

That surprised some of my leadership team, including Steve Riddell, who led the design project management of our new office.

"I was shocked at the level of detail that I did not believe he would want to get into, for example, naming the rooms. He drove me crazy. But he was very deep into the detail, and in some cases, he would hold things up, because the end result was more important to him than the time frame to get there. And that frustrates guys like me who just want to get it done," Steve said. "But he's an incredibly intense thinker. And it's that thinking process that has enabled him to move forward in a variety of areas that other people wouldn't have gone."

As Jerry Seinfeld told *Harvard Business Review* editors, *Seinfeld* "was successful because I micromanaged it—every word, every line, every take, every edit, every casting." Understand that this doesn't mean you should micromanage everything. What it means is that culture begins with the leader. Period. In my case, our office design was something I, like Jerry, felt needed to be micromanaged. Within these walls, every day, hundreds of people spend hours away from their loved ones. They labor to grow this business and put food on their tables. It is your direct obligation, and not one that should ever be delegated, to ensure your culture is evident on every surface, bearing evidence of your core values. As CEO, you're also Chief *Environmental* Officer.

If an employee is in the call center on the phone with an unhappy customer, I want them to look up and see **Enjoy the Ride** painted on the wall in front of them. I want them to be reminded that what we're doing should be fun—helping people improve their homes and their lives. If they aren't having fun, they can take a break at the foosball table or brew a mocha from one of the many fancy coffee machines Steve Riddell convinced me to buy years ago. Wait, that's not right. He never asked. He just did it.

Zoogle

My conviction about the office environment developed over time and was influenced by a number of corporate innovators, including Google, Apple, Zappos, and Pixar.

I visited Google in California and New York. I saw lots of color; lots of glass; people interacting; people having fun; interesting, creative things that were unexpectedly paired with high tech. I always felt that GCC should be a combination of creativity, color, openness, and data. If you want to have creative and unrestrained thinking, you need to have a creative, unrestrained environment. Environments must be conducive to your objectives. For instance, if you want to grow cacti, you put them in the desert, not in Hawaii. It is also my strong belief that to understand the future, you need to understand and respect the past. Our environment respected the past, with a hearty dose of artifacts, but was high-tech enough to encourage thinking about the future.

The Launchpad at the Global Custom Commerce Office

At Zappos, I observed that they had themes for each row in the contact center. I liked the idea that in one place it might be a jungle, while a few yards away it was canoes. Google does the same thing. That allows for individuality among associates. It reflects our diverse staff and audience. It clearly says, "What we're doing is different."

Google's New York office had a lot of designs related to New York, which prompted me to do the same thing, but related to our history and our culture. As I've referenced before, each room in our office is named for a critical person or part of our history. They are meant to help me tell the story every day to every associate of how we came to be where we are. That keeps us rooted in our past as we stretch into the future.

One way we do that is by taking all new associates on a bus tour to see the different offices we've inhabited over the years, beginning with

The Alley, to show them how far we've come. That resonates with a lot of our team.

"When you go from sixty-eight associates to three hundred fifty associates, you're bringing on new people all the time. How do you retain that culture?" noted Larry. "It was really important for him to educate people on where we came from, not just telling them about it, but taking them out to the places where the company started, having a ten-page quiz on the history of the company, and having new people have to find the answers by asking people.

"I remember once we took the whole company, and all of us crowded into the alley. And that was a great experience, because everybody's there together, and you're all talking about and hearing from people like Sharon and Ann, the very first two associates."

That trip Larry references happened in 2013, one week before we moved the company to one of the coolest offices in America. I never lost sight of where we came from, and knowing those beginnings—the windowless, dumpster-scented back room at The Alley—reminds our people what you can achieve when you work together. It's why, when you visit GCC's offices, the very first space you enter is our grandest artifact, designed to look like The Alley, graffiti and all (though thankfully without the rotting Chinese food aroma). We had a movie set firm design and build it.

It's also why street signs hang from the ceiling, named after critical people and places in our development, including *Naomi Way* and *Barbara Boulevard*, which intersected right outside my office.

That resonated with Kevin Hofmann, who was Home Depot's president of its online division at the time of our merger, and who later also assumed the title of CMO: "He made me a better leader. One thing I always remembered about him is his passion for symbolism. He was always thinking about the next couple of years, while he honored the past. Your organization watches you. Your organization needs to understand where you're going, and symbolism is important."

All this careful environmental craftsmanship is not just for the benefit of your associates and others who venture into your environment. Don't forget yourself. It's so easy to start taking your past for granted. A main purpose of conspicuously highlighting the past was to keep myself humble; to stay hungry and not take our success for granted.

As an additional reinforcement, every computer I've ever used since The Alley, almost twenty-five years ago, has a picture of The Alley as my wallpaper background. So, every day when I went to work, I *passed* through it.

You Need This Meeting

Google is also where I first conceived of the idea of the SayJay meetings, which I launched in 2007, when we had about 115 associates. Google's founders, Sergey Brin and Larry Page, met with the company every week on a livestream. I thought, if a huge company like Google can turn off its phones every week to hold an all-hands meeting, we can, too.

So, from exactly 2:00 to 2:15 p.m. every Thursday, everyone in the company stops what they're doing. There's a voice message that activates on the phones to tell callers we're in training, and the team stands together and talks. Well, I did most of the talking. That's why it's called SayJay.

At the time I started the all-hands meetings, JustBlinds.com, which we'd acquired just two years prior, was in a different building thirty minutes across town, and many of the associates in that building had never met those in GCC's office. People can't collaborate if they aren't connected. So, I used Skype to video conference everyone together for fifteen minutes, which was considered very high tech in 2007.

"It not only allowed us to work together better, it saved our culture," Daniel said. "You can't keep a culture between two offices, even though they were both in Houston. It was so important to have everyone together at times. Essential."

It's so essential, we continued our weekly SayJays every week for thirteen years even through the COVID-19 pandemic, connecting everyone remotely.

SayJay topics change each week, but leadership usually calls out people for special achievements, highlights associate anniversaries, notes charity events we're sponsoring, and mentions other feel-good mainstays. We discuss the results of our fearless experiments—good, bad, and ugly. Most important, we prepare for what's coming. Honesty about change is the single best thing you can do to gain your team's buy-in for what's ahead and develop their resilience and adaptability. It's your job as a leader to make sure everybody knows what's expected and what the future holds.

RULES FOR AN EFFECTIVE ALL-HANDS MEETING

1. Start and end on time. No exceptions.
2. Nothing is off limits.
3. Be candid, especially about challenges you see ahead.

SayJays are also about introducing new hires to the team and giving them a chance to express themselves with vulnerability, by either singing, telling a joke, dancing, or performing in some way. Many of the new associates are hilarious (in a good way!), many are extraordinarily talented, and others should just be admired for doing anything at all. It was my and many others' favorite part of SayJays. Outsiders who witness a SayJay get an instant, concentrated dose of our core values and culture. You'll see people **expressing themselves**, discussing their **experimentation** in an effort to **Evolve Continuously**, all while having fun and **Enjoying the Ride**.

Interestingly, after Google's influence on our culture, my older son, Craig, was recruited by Google when he worked for our HR department. He worked at Google for five years before leaving to join, what else, a startup.

It's Not About Ping-Pong

An effective environment doesn't necessarily mean colorful offices and foosball. It can mean stark, even miserly fixtures. The Alley, where we started, didn't even have a real desk. It's the energy of how people behave inside the office that matters.

Our next move after The Alley wasn't much better, but it *was* our first legitimate office. On Beechnut Street in Houston, it was across the street from a Lowe's and over a Subway sandwich shop. We had maybe 1,500 square feet to start with, but to Sharon, Ann, and me, it was palatial. Plus, anytime a tenant left an adjacent office, we took over their lease.

Over the years in that space, we took over three or four different offices adjacent to ours, and when we outgrew those, we moved downstairs to the first floor where there was some retail space. We put our IT and Accounting departments there. It seemed thrilling to me to be on two floors, but what I didn't realize was that the poor folks who worked downstairs, though they had plenty of sunlight, felt they were relegated to the basement. You know that scene in the movie *Office Space* when Milton gets his red stapler taken away? That's how they felt.

When we first moved in, I bought all used furniture. We were a startup with no money, and that meant everyone needed to know how scrappy and judicious we were going to be with funds. The environment should be designed for the intended mindset you want.

In fact, that's the office, Three Brainer Tower, we were in when I interviewed Larry.

"I was at a mortgage company," Larry remembered, "and a friend I worked with told me about an opportunity running the Technology department for a local startup. They were looking for someone doing Java, and he was a Microsoft guy, so he said, 'Why don't you go talk to him?' It was the biggest mistake he ever made."

Okay, so Larry *may* have been put off by the condition of Three Brainer Tower.

"I was driving around going, 'This can't possibly be right. I don't see any office building.' And finally I figured out it was in this strip mall where there was a trophy shop and a diner," Larry remembered. "And I went in, and I went upstairs, and I wandered down this long, dark hallway. And it's just a door. There was no sign on it. It's this just mess of a floor, with blinds stuff everywhere, brochures—it was just chaos."

And yet, here was Larry, this tech extraordinaire who had worked for JPMorgan Chase and National Australia Bank, not deterred at all.

"I'm a little comfortable with that environment because I grew up in a very entrepreneurial family business, where my desk was some cardboard boxes with a wooden door across the top. So I wasn't scared when I saw this environment. I thought, maybe there's a lot of opportunity here in a startup."

Culture is top down, without a doubt, but it's not a dictatorship. My core values are infused everywhere in GCC, but our people bring them to life.

As Steve Riddell said, "People think about culture as being whether you give free food or not. It just has nothing to do with that."

Initially, what attracted Home Depot to GCC was that we were killing them in blind sales. They were looking to acquire a company that had developed a pricing engine for blinds. There were virtually no online blind sales for Home Depot and we were at that time doing $115 million.

Home Depot had also tried to create their own configuration engine, and it was already too expensive, not much had been completed, the prospect of it was too uncertain, and there was no confidence in the timeline and final cost. We had Larry and Tim hard at work on Autobahn at the time. When it was ready, a classic make-or-buy decision arose. Home Depot decided to buy.

"We had a good in-store blinds business, but we didn't have a well-developed online blinds business yet," said HD Online President Kevin Hofmann. "Like most big companies, we had trouble getting out of our own way sometimes. Next thing you know, we're looking at a $10 million or $20 million project to build this, and who are these people who are going to build it? They've never done it before, and they tell me it's going to take a year, so it's probably going to take three years. Three years is an eternity. The world changes in three years.

"We basically said, 'If we want to change the game with online blind selling, we probably shouldn't try to build it ourselves.'"

When you have a new product or service, many believe that companies with the same or a similar product or service are not good sales prospects. But those who have tried to build something and, in some way, failed are many times better prospects. First, they clearly want what you have, and second, they appreciate how hard it was to create. They may be relieved you can bail them out of their substandard situation.

After the merger, Home Depot wanted us to implement Autobahn on their site. We had the privilege of integrating Autobahn for one of the largest retailers on the planet, and we experienced a big boost in sales as a result—as did Home Depot.

Once we proved the benefits of Autobahn, we extended the technology to other hard-to-buy product categories for Home Depot, such as custom decks, storm doors, countertops, and more. We built it first online, using the world's first *Pipfigurator.* Seth coined that term by combining the words "configurator" and "PIP." PIP is an acronym for Product Information Page, which is where a product's basic information is described on a website. The term stuck, and people throughout Home Depot began using it in everyday conversation. Every time they did, Seth and I would glance at each other and give a little nod and a bit of a smile, probably only detectable to us.

We had thought we could make such a difference, but it did not come without its detractors. Who were we to have the audacity to think we could do things that could not be done by the thousands of highly skilled and capable engineers and product managers at Home Depot's corporate office in Atlanta?

It wasn't that we were smarter. We had a different mindset, and we were determined to experiment in incremental ways in the customers' best interests. Our merger meant we could combine the technology and entrepreneurial mindset of GCC with the formidable platform of Home Depot. It was as if GCC was Tony Stark and Home Depot was J.A.R.V.I.S. and Tony's suit, and together we would form Iron Man. Or, it was as if GCC added one tiny drop of magic potion into the enormous vat that was Home Depot. That drop would barely tint the contents of the vat, but most stakeholders would know it was there. These are ways I helped motivate our team and encourage us to persevere. When your team doubts themselves, it is your responsibility to remind them that you believe in them and they have permission to fail, but never to give up.

So, sure, Home Depot loved what they saw as it related to our sales and Autobahn. That's what drew them in. But when they saw the culture, they understood it was why we were able to, with so few dollars and so few people, develop something that Home Depot and everyone else had not been able to.

Home Depot could buy technology, or they could buy technology *with* people who were able to build and augment it, and do other things within Home Depot. Culture played a big part in why they bought us, even though that was not their original intent. It certainly added to the valuation.

With the merger on the horizon, it was also especially important to me to make sure that the senior leadership team and I wouldn't leave. If you've got a culture where everybody loves what they're doing, it's quite beneficial for a potential acquirer to think, "We don't want this company to dissolve or for the culture to become less than what it is. We need to make sure we don't screw it up."

The Justice League Eats Together

Communication is critical to culture, and how you communicate should be determined by your core values. If we proclaim that one of our core values is to **Express Yourself**, then, by God, our office space should be set up to encourage that, our meetings should focus on hearing everyone's voice, and our policies should allow for individual expression.

Along those lines, I set up our entire office to encourage accidental interactions, something I learned from Steve Jobs of Apple and Tony Hsieh at Zappos. They believed, as I do, that in designing a building, it is important not to pigeonhole people and sequester them by department.

So, in our building, we put popular places, such as the dining areas, in the center, where everyone gathers, prompting sudden collisions of people from different departments. It's important for people to know there are others in the organization beyond their small team or deskmates—they need to see them, have a chance to ask them what they're working on, and even offer advice or assistance from their perspective, which is different but operating within the same core values and mission.

Multi-departmental gatherings also remind us that we're part of something larger, and that each group's goals and initiatives are one part of our total enterprise. Further, knowing more about the whole organism casts a wider net for innovation and continuous evolution—how often has someone outside your industry offered you an outsider's suggestion that is brilliant because it comes from a different way of thinking? Commingling our teams as much as possible creates a Justice League of sorts, with Wonder Women helping Supermen and vice versa.

And finally, constantly mixing people from different departments helps them understand how their roles affect others. And that's important. Everyone wants to know where they fit in and how they make a difference. It's another reason the weekly SayJays are essential, even when I am no longer a part of them.

For instance, during the COVID-19 pandemic, it was more critical than ever to connect our teams. All associates were working remotely, and that could easily lead to a disconnect between departments—no one to bump into on the way to refill your coffee mug. That's why our weekly SayJays during that time included updates from department heads, sharing the successes and challenges we faced. We also shared photos and funny videos of our associates working (or trying to) from home to keep the jovial atmosphere typical with our SayJays.

Allowing your employees to work from home is an interesting topic within the subject of corporate culture. After all the time I devoted to creating an office space that demonstrated our culture in every nook and cranny, and designing said office to force interdepartmental interactions among associates, you may be surprised to know I was an early advocate for telecommuting.

Throughout my career, about 25 percent of my time has been spent working from home. I especially benefited from that when I needed to think without distractions. An open-door policy only works when the door is open, which invites precious and unplanned interactions with associates. At the same time, if you are working on solving a critical issue or refining corporate strategy, frequent interruptions will slow you down and likely decrease the quality of your outcome. You owe your employees your best work. That means spending some of it in solitude.

I believe the same is true for my associates, and I put it into practice in 2010, at which time about 20 percent of our workforce regularly worked from home. When COVID-19 swept the world, many companies were forced to try remote work for the first time with no notice. That's a very challenging proposition in the best of times, and life-threatening for your company in the worst. And crises are always the worst. In our case, everyone was already prepared to work from home, and business went on without a hitch.

I've said it before, but it's continually an important lesson: every leader needs to think about the unthinkable, when a fire, earthquake, disease outbreak, or any other wide-scale disruption could bring your company as you know it to a halt. Remote work gives you instant alternate locations should your physical space no longer be an option.

4 TIPS TO MAKE WORK FROM HOME WORK FOR YOU AND YOUR PEOPLE

1. **Trust, yet verify.**
   Set clear, objective metrics to be met, no matter where your associates work. If they are not met, the associate loses the privilege to work from home until they are. Remote work won't go perfectly on your first try, but don't give up. Make adjustments and provide the infrastructure and support your team needs to reach its goals.

2. **Create seamless connections.**
   When remote work is truly working, customers should never know where an associate is. Ensure that your IT team configures all communication systems to seamlessly integrate remote-work employees. Customers must get the same great service.

3. **Communication is king.**
   Everyone needs to work at creating effortless communication. They must report to weekly all-hands meetings, livestreamed to all employees. Managers should maintain frequent—daily or weekly—video conversations and coaching with their teams, both one-on-one and as a group to maintain culture and connection.

4. **Don't disappear.**
   Require, when possible, all associates to come into the office at least once per week to touch base in person. Absence makes the heart grow fonder, but extended absence makes a culture grow weaker. This could be your all-hands meeting or a departmental staff meeting. This also allows all employees to meet in person, so new associates don't feel disconnected from some team members.

Make Gratitude Part of Your Culture

Another way I communicate with associates is through expressions of gratitude. We don't offer snacks and free food because it's a talent retention tool. We do it for the same reason we invite guests to our home: we are thankful for them and want to enjoy our time together with sustenance.

I took great joy in our holiday parties every year, especially in surprising associates with a special gift. One stands out to Barbara.

"He decided he wanted everybody to have their own personalized bobblehead of themselves," she said, recalling a holiday party from years past. At the time, we employed about seventy people. "I was so impressed with Jay's creativity and desire to think of a themed gift that would be symbolic to each person's contribution to the company. Together they were the Blinds.com family. They were viewed as integral to the company's success. It really spoke volumes to me about Jay."

It was expensive and difficult to pull off. I asked Dixie, who is also a professional photographer, to snap a photo of every associate under the guise of taking portraits for a company directory. I used a California company to produce the bobbleheads, all wearing a Superman or Superwoman costume, then put each one in a shoebox and wrapped the boxes in paper that looked like bricks. When stacked at the event center for the party, it just looked like a brick wall.

I wore a suit to the party that night, and during my comments, I told my staff that they were each a superhero, and pulled open my shirt to reveal a Superman T-shirt underneath. Everyone opened their box at that moment. It was one of my favorite experiences and why we named one of our meeting rooms in our new building "Bobbleheads."

I love gift giving. For me, it's merging a clever idea with immense gratitude to communicate feelings that can't be verbalized effectively.

Send in the Dogs

As your company grows, it is likely you will hire more and more experienced—and thus expensive—talent. But there's a saying that something is only expensive if it doesn't work. It's usually used to reference advertising, but the same goes for talent.

You will move from potentially shabby offices to sleek, modern digs. You will have more money to spend on amenities for your employees. You may even dress better and drive a fancier car. Do this, but do not, for one second, lose your sense of self or your company's culture in that natural transition. It's easy to do, so always be mindful.

This loss of self and loss of value placed on company culture is one of the reasons leaders get the reputation of being jerks. We feel the stakes are higher, even if they're not; we listen to people who weren't part of building our business and who don't know our culture; and we forget one of the most important core values: **Enjoy the Ride**. When Morgan Stanley invested in us, which they did a couple years before our merger with Home Depot, they brought more professionalism to the way we operated, including the style and substance of our presentations. Morgan Stanley naturally had a lot more experience in creating business presentations than we did. Of course, we took their guidance, but we also knew that what we had done up to that point had worked well for us—and was aligned with our core values.

Bobby Bassman, one of the two principals with Morgan Stanley Expansion Capital charged with evaluating and pursuing GCC along with Lincoln Isetta, recalls, "The first time I met Jay and Daniel, they gave me their pitch deck. Lincoln and I thought, 'They've got a great business, but their deck is really bad.'"

Bobby and Lincoln's perspective of our poorly written presentation skills didn't stop there. A year later, when Daniel and I were asked by

Lowe's to discuss a partnership, we faced a crossroads with our investors. We had a great idea for our partnership: an e-commerce station within Lowe's stores for all configurable products where a family could come in and choose some type of custom project, such as blinds or a gazebo, or even something as simple as a doghouse. At this station, using the doghouse example, they could choose the roof, the colors, and the materials, and our technology would visualize it and create a list of all the parts needed, as well as a map showing where all the items were located in the store. It also would dynamically create instructions based on what had been configured, and also give the buyer access to roofing, siding, and painting professionals based in a centralized location in the United States. The purchase would also create social media that could be sent to all the buyer's friends.

This was in 2012, when an interconnected retail omni-channel was barely being talked about. While Morgan Stanley supported the idea, they were aghast about the cartoon illustrations we used to present it, which included Homer D. Poe, the longtime handyman mascot for Home Depot inside a doghouse, his dirty orange apron lying on the ground due to his conquest by Lowe's.

Our investors at Morgan Stanley could not have been more opposed to us including those cartoon illustrations. They thought it was unprofessional; we thought it was great salesmanship. Against their advice, we left the cartoon in and the Lowe's executives loved it. In fact, we got a standing ovation at that point. Robert Gfeller, who was senior vice president of customer experience at the time, looked at all the other people from Lowe's in the room and said, "You got to work a deal with them."

Interestingly, we soon got a chance to test the efficacy of that last slide again, when Home Depot called us out of the blue and asked us to discuss a partnership. This time, we put Lowe's in the doghouse at the end and, again, received a great ovation.

Putting Lowe's® in the Doghouse Presentation

We followed our culture, we followed our gut, and when we ultimately merged with Home Depot, Bobby and Lincoln sent me a toy doghouse with Lowe's stickers on it and a dog called "Bob" inside. I still have that as a trophy in my office, and I smile whenever I see it. We even named a conference room "the Dog House," with the slides from that presentation framed and prominently displayed on the walls, along with chew toys and water bowls, to remind us to stay true to ourselves and our sense of humor. Along with a sense of humor, there are ways to lift spirits and make working fun. Here are eleven of them.

11 EASY WAYS TO MAKE WORK FUN*

1. Have a "decorate your area" contest. Give each employee a nominal decorating allowance and challenge them to decorate on a theme. Or encourage departments to develop an overall theme: Our Customer Service department hangs extreme sports equipment from the ceiling—reminding us all that we go to extremes for our customers. Our Accounting department chose a pirate theme, since they're always looking for buried treasure.
2. Use color to brighten your office space. Paint is cheap—and cheery.
3. Hang movie posters on your walls, with employees' faces replacing those of the real movie stars. It can be a great motivator!
4. Celebrate holidays with parties: a Mardi Gras krewe parade through the office, a cookout on the premises, a carnival.
5. Celebrate success with dessert or other food. Most of us think eating together is fun! Not to mention the appeal of free food.
6. Have silly dress-up days: Halloween, Super Bowl, "My Favorite College" Day, "Bring Your Pet/Kids/Parents to Work" Day.
7. Smile. When you, as the leader, are in a bad mood, everyone is in a bad mood. ("When Mama ain't happy, ain't nobody happy.") Be happy.
8. Put games in the break room or lunchroom. I moved my Ping-Pong table to the office. Set up a chess set for a continuing game. Jigsaw puzzles especially work well.

9. Invite your employees to dance and sing, and then create a video, such as our numerous lip dubs you can find on YouTube online.
10. Hire a photographer to roam your office one day and make a slideshow of the resulting photos. Display it in your reception area or lunchroom.
11. Create fun garb. When our IT department began work on a major initiative that helped propel our growth significantly faster, we called it Autobahn. Everyone on the team received a personalized racing mechanic's uniform.

*This list was first published in my most-read blog on Inc.com, *11 Easy Ways to Make Work Fun.*

What Are You Really Saying?

Above all, communication should be clear and direct. It's something my son Craig learned from me that he says has aided him in his leadership roles.

"If I'm writing an email, it's probably five sentences or less. And it's probably going to tell you exactly what I need in bold print, so I can make it very easy for the user," he said. "It's about knowing your audience and knowing how to influence that audience by understanding what's intrinsically motivating to them. That's something my dad's really good at and something that I try to emulate."

Finally, keep in mind that, as the leader, you are always communicating something. As I learned from my speaking coach, Michael

Allosso, "you cannot *not* communicate." If your office door is shut, it communicates secrecy. Sometimes, that's unavoidable. Okay. But if you shut your door for a prolonged amount of time, it can be unsettling to associates. That's why I had the entire front of my office made completely of see-through glass. Nothing to hide, even when the door was shut.

If you keep your head down and rush into the office each day without making eye contact or exchanging pleasantries with associates, you are communicating that something is wrong. Or that you don't care about those people. Absent information, people usually imagine the worst.

If you keep to yourself and avoid speaking to staff, they may feel you are communicating displeasure with the job they're doing or that you're not engaged in the company or, worse yet, that you consider yourself above the day-to-day.

And if you are constantly working, sending emails at all hours of the night, in at 6:00 a.m. and out at 9:00 p.m., you are communicating that that's the expectation for everyone. Also not great. While my family will tell you that I worked all the time, the truth is that while I may have been *thinking* about work most of the time, I wasn't physically in the office or engaging with associates during that time. I've always wanted associates to have a healthy balance, to be able to experiment and evolve and enjoy their lives outside of work so they can bring that attitude to the office. I'm pleased that Seth, our Chief Digital Officer, saw that and emulated it with his team.

"We don't want people to compete with each other, like, 'I was here at 5:00 a.m., and I left at 7:00 p.m.' I don't think anybody in leadership supports that. We would ask, 'Why are you doing that? That can't be good. You're not creating value by doing that.'

"I expect you to fit work into life, not life into work. And you need to find that balance, and you need to come to your leader if you need help to figure out how. Because if you don't, then I'm not going to be getting what I'm paying for when you are here. Jay supports that."

I had to take a hard look at what I was communicating by being my naturally introverted, intense self. I had to consciously display to my team that I was living my core values, namely **Enjoying the Ride**. I made sure I seemed at ease in the office; I walked around and chatted with folks; I smiled and joked no matter what stress I was feeling. And I never yelled.

That's something I had to teach myself—to control my outward appearance. Esther remembers me as a "yeller" while she was growing up, and I suppose that's true. Craig took notice of this change in me, as well, when he worked in our HR department. He had to reconcile the person he knew as Dad with the CEO of GCC.

"At the company, he was much more outgoing," Craig recalled. "He's good at flexing the outgoing, social, gregarious nature of what it takes to be a CEO or the type of CEO he aspires to be, which is a man of the people, so to speak. At home, he is much more internal, a little bit more inward, a lot quieter, a lot less outgoing and talkative. The intensity is still there. The intensity earlier on was a little bit more, you could say unbridled, and I think he was able to, over time, get better about controlling his temper. I think he got better about keeping that restrained and using that energy in a more productive way, to where if there's feedback, it can be direct, but it wasn't done in an aggressive way."

Craig added, "That just came with learning and life experiences. Losing my mom and his wife obviously played a big role in some of that."

Loss, Love, and Gadflies

And that will always be true. Esther was only thirteen, Craig eleven, and Alec six, when Naomi was diagnosed. That was five years before her death, and it was a very serious initial diagnosis. By the time she found a lump, it had already spread to her lymph nodes.

Naomi never wanted the children to know how sick she actually was. Even weeks before her death, we never told them she was dying of cancer. I'm not sure they'll ever forgive me for that, and I do regret the decision. But at the time, I wanted to do whatever Naomi wanted to do because I wanted to bring her comfort in any way I could. This was important to her, so I honored her wishes, knowing it would give her peace of mind to give her children more of a chance to enjoy their childhoods and not worry about her.

Esther was eighteen when her mother died, just about to go to Boston University. Craig was sixteen, in high school, considering colleges and playing competitive tennis. Alec was eleven. I was lost without her. So were they.

I made mistakes. No question. I had no family nearby to lean on, three devastated and hurt children, and a business taking off. That period of my life is a blur, but what I can remember is that after taking care of both my dad and wife, and having the sole responsibility for raising three children while building a business, I couldn't do it all. I needed help and thought I needed a wife. My marriage to Naomi had been wonderful and I wanted to re-create what we had. Within two years, I remarried.

But life doesn't work that way. It was a disaster. The marriage lasted less than two years, but I knew within months I'd made a major error of judgment. My children were deeply and adversely affected by it, perhaps most of all Alec, who, as the youngest, was stuck alone in a new household while I was busy at work and his siblings were at college.

We divorced, and a year later, I met Barbara. I fell in love with her quickly and my children seemed happy for me, but by then I had learned to move slower. Plus, with all that I had been through, I didn't want it to seem to Barbara that I was rebounding. Her son, Ted, was still in high school; her daughter, Jenny, was in college; and Barbara herself had just been in a twenty-five-year marriage that had ended less than two years earlier. So, we both wanted to take things slowly.

Our mutual friend, Susan, connected us, and it was one of the glorious times in my life. Barbara and I were both at the same Shabbat group, one that continues to meet one Friday a month, even fifteen years later. Susan pointed her out, standing in the kitchen with friends, and I walked over, eager to make a good first impression, and said, "Hi, I'm Jay Steinfeld, and I understand we're supposed to meet."

Then I shook her hand firmly.

"He really swept me off my feet," Barbara said, smiling. "I just liked that he was so direct."

So, we began our courtship, slowly and gently, but always directly. From the moment I met her, I knew she was special, and I didn't want anything or anyone to get in the way of that. But I had learned the value of patience, like letting a freshly opened wine breathe.

"I remember the first time we went out, I said, 'Why don't I just meet you there?'" Barbara remembered. "I was thinking about my son and didn't know how he would react to someone coming to the house to take me out. When we began dating, I also was thinking about Alec and all he had been through with the loss of his mother and a brief second marriage. For both of our youngest who were still living at home, I was very happy to take things slow. I'm so glad we did. Neither of us needed to feel pressure."

Barbara and I dated for six years. We began seeing each other before the business surged, but it was beginning to show signs of things going in a good direction.

"We would have fun doing all kinds of different things from just hanging out to being with our families or with friends. One weekend in particular, Jay suggested we go to the Trinity Lutheran Church near downtown, where they were doing a weekend of Ella Fitzgerald's jazz, culminating in their Sunday service dedicated to her as well. It was a new and great experience," Barbara said. When you're in your fifties, six years is a long time to wait if you're serious about each other. With both of us valuing family as we did, we knew timing was important. And that's one of the reasons Barbara and I love each other. It's because of our appreciation and love for our own families, as well as the appreciation we have for each other's family. We give each other space and time to be with our family, although the best time is when we're all together.

We decided we wouldn't marry until the last child, Alec, was off to college at NYU. Once that happened, I knew it was time.

We went to Sorrento, a Houston restaurant we both really liked. I had concocted another experiment, having reserved a table for two right next to the pianist. That night they had a violinist accompanying the pianist. That's because I hired the violinist ahead of time to be there so they could play a duet of a classical piece by Russian composer Dmitri Shostakovich called "Romance" from the *Gadfly Suite* that she and I both really liked.

When they played it, Barbara turned to me and said, "Hey, don't we know that song?"

I said, "Yeah, that's the song we both really like." Then I got down on one knee.

Thankfully she said yes, which made everything afterward go so much better.

The restaurant guests applauded. Then our kids, who had been patiently waiting outside, walked in, single file, to join us for dinner. At the end of the line was her dad, whom I'd flown in from Kansas City. It was really special for him to be there.

Barbara was elated. We all went into a back wine room I had reserved, with a big round table. We had a delicious, festive dinner and talked about how wonderful everything was. It went just perfectly.

The proposal's timing was important to me because my daughter Esther's wedding was imminent, and after all those years together with Barbara, it was important that relatives and friends at Esther's wedding perceived Barbara as my fiancée—to me, an important distinction from a significant other. I didn't want to have that announcement diminish Esther's big day, however, so I asked Esther and, as expected, she was completely on board. The proposal both surprised and delighted Barbara. After six years together, we married on November 23, 2012.

Marrying Barbara was very much me following **the 4 Es**. She still helps me **Evolve Continuously**, marriage is the epitome of an **Experiment Without Fear of Failure**, and marrying her was clearly me **Expressing Myself** and the great love I have for her. And every day since, I've been **Enjoying the Ride**.

IN SYSTEMS WE TRUST
How to Scale Beyond the Startup Phase

*No matter how brilliant your mind or strategy, if you're
playing a solo game, you'll always lose out to a team.*

—Reid Hoffman

One thing that allowed GCC to continue thriving after our merger, which, according to common belief, should have thwarted our innovation and stymied our culture, was the work I had done for years to scale decision-making throughout our organization.

That started with my transformation from solopreneur to small business owner to CEO of a large enterprise who understood the need for and value of delegation. As my leadership team became stronger and more effective, I encouraged them to make more of the critical decisions in our organization. (Some had already been doing this, as Larry had when he began tinkering with the idea for Autobahn.) Building a company is not just about growing sales, but also building an infrastructure and the processes that enable the company to evolve on its own without you. And without constantly needing you to nudge its people. I refer to it as *autonomous excellence*. It was gratifying and fulfilling (and a relief!) to watch excellence materialize without my direct involvement. One of my children, eleven at the time, once asked me what I do as CEO. I replied, "I set the vision and culture, get the right people, and ensure they execute." He replied in a matter-of-fact manner, "So you don't do any *real* work?"

Maybe not. To create *autonomous excellence* so your business can scale without you, first decide how your company will make decisions.

Decide How to Decide

Scaling decision-making is not just about letting other people make decisions. As with building trust in employees through incremental delegation of tasks, you need to establish a process for how decisions are made in your business and have an organizational design to support that. You also need a culture that says it's OK for your leaders to make decisions without always first running it up the flagpole.

Without that, you're going to be a bottleneck in your own growth.

It also doesn't mean removing yourself entirely from the decision-making process. It's critical to stay involved in every aspect of the business, but you must trust the people you have put in charge. For instance, randomly attend department meetings. You'll learn what's being prioritized, but also who is speaking up and who is just agreeing with the leader. Are your leaders seeking input by asking insightful, curious questions, coaching, and not making declarations? If not, you have a coaching opportunity.

Stay involved by getting regular reports from your leaders and through frequent one-to-one meetings. Schedule time with your direct reports and ensure that they do the same with theirs. Ask questions and learn what's getting in their way and how you can help. If you think you don't have time for monthly meetings, or don't need them because you talk with your staff often, you're wrong. These meetings give a structure to the conversation and allow you to understand the feelings and thought processes of your team. These types of discussions rarely happen without consistently setting aside uninterrupted time.

Keep your organization flat—i.e., limited hierarchy—otherwise, by the time information reaches you, it might be too late. Even with a flat organization, it's almost certain the information is getting filtered along the way. Make sure people at all levels are comfortable going straight to the top, but when they do, suggest they do so only after telling their direct supervisor and including them in the discussion—unless, of course, there's impropriety. You must have a way for people to let you know when things are afoul.

That also includes open-door meetings for all departments, with very few exceptions. If someone wants to sit in on an R&D meeting and learn what new things we're working on, great. That's something my executive assistant, Shannon, who's worked in multiple areas of our company, thrives on.

"I get to learn about every single aspect of the business that I wouldn't be able to touch if I was doing anything else. It's an environment where you're constantly learning," Shannon said.

It took me years to learn to hand over some of the decisions and trust my team. Shannon, who joined our company in 2007, remembers a very different Jay back then.

"Initially, he was very much a micromanager," she said. "Over the years, he really let the people who are running a department run things. Now, granted, he still had questions, but overall, he learned to let things go and be hands-off."

Removing yourself from the minutiae of the day-to-day allows you to be the most helpful to your team by seeing the big picture of what's ahead and how the different areas of your company could work better together. For example, I realized near the end of my tenure that we had a problem with training Design Consultants in our call center, what we refer to as the Customer Engagement Center (CEC).

New GCC associates are incubated and closely trained in the ILIAD, which is a training program we developed and stands for Institute for Learning, Innovation, Advancement, and Development. New associates must go through this program before they get on the phones full-time. That's great, but at one point, it was taking fully two months from their first day before we were unleashing them independently on the phones. I stepped in to help the department head trim that down, realizing that, while the intention was good, we were trying to teach them too much all at once. I worked with the team to implement changes, where we would teach new hires through first grade, so to speak, then let them take first-grade phone calls, gradually scaling up until they could handle anything. Now we're getting people on the phones in just two weeks, instead of two months.

Data vs. Instinct

As a leader, making decisions is one of your top responsibilities. There are times you need to make a snap judgment based on limited data and some instinct, and there are many more times when you need data and time to make the right call. The trick is to know the difference.

"He makes decisions quickly," noted Steve O'Connor. "The worst thing for an organization is to not make a decision. You paralyze everybody. There are times when you should do A-B testing, and other times if it's common sense, we should just do it, and we'll pull it back if it doesn't work. That need for speed versus paralyzing yourself with data—he's got the right balance."

Balance is difficult. On the one hand, data is powerful. On the other hand, your instincts have gotten you to where you are. While you want to empower your leadership team and you hope you have painted a compelling vision, sometimes you just have to trust yourself above all others. Larry said it best: "The senior leadership team was involved in the decision process, but sometimes, regardless of the logic we applied or the analysis we did, he would go with his gut.

"A specific example was when we moved to the new building. We were in kind of a dilapidated building. We had decent furniture, but it really wasn't that nice. We were debating—do we move or do we stay? And the whole team looked at the finances and, because we were trying to grow and get our [profit] to a certain point, we decided we're not going to move at this point. We all agreed on that.

"Then we came in the next morning, and Jay says, 'We're going to get the new place; we're going to buy a whole bunch of really nice furniture. We need the space; we're going to grow.'

"We didn't have solid data that indicated we absolutely were going to grow, but Jay said, 'No, we're going to grow. People are going to come talk to us, they're going to want to partner with us, acquire us, there's going to be things that are going on, and we need to be in the right building; we need to have the right image.'"

At the time we were discussing whether or not to move again, we were at Four and Five Brainer Towers, which were housed in the same building on Rogerdale Road, about half a mile west of where the

141

GCC offices are now. We had space on the second floor—Four Brainer Tower—but again, we grew and needed to take over the rest of the first floor, which we called Five Brainer Tower. We were growing consistently, and I knew we needed a home that would be able to handle that growth.

We moved to 10255 Richmond Ave., a nondescript Class-B building, which, at first, housed all of us on the third floor. We named one of the conference rooms Six Brainer Tower to pay homage to our history. Then we grew to the fourth floor, and a conference room there became Seven Brainer Tower. Then we added the second floor and dubbed one of its conference rooms Eight Brainer Tower. If people dismissed the coolness of our office from the outside, that changed when they stepped off the elevator.

The journey matters. Keeping that ritual helped our associates stay connected to our past and think about the future—where would Nine Brainer Tower be? In our 2020 Vision pamphlet, you can see an illustration of our future campus, and if you look carefully, you'll see Billion Brainer Tower. **Enjoying the Ride**, even when no one could see it.

"And then we built this space. And Home Depot came along, and they're like, 'Wow, this company is amazing,'" Larry said. "I think it's very likely that if we had been in the old building in the old environment, they wouldn't have acquired us, or the multiple they paid for us would have been significantly lower. I think they were so wowed by the environment that we had built here. It was a big investment, but I think it paid off."

Here's my advice on how to achieve that critical balance in decision-making.

5 TIMES YOU SHOULD TAKE IT SLOW

1. Be slow with your strategic planning. Figure out, slowly and carefully, what you want to do, then shift into high gear.
2. Be slow to criticize and quick to appreciate.
3. Be slow to make judgments, especially when one person calls out another. Get all the information before concluding.
4. Be slow to move something to the top of your list. There's folly in making everything a priority.
5. Be slow to hire. Our interviewees go through at least five rounds of intensive interviews with multiple leaders and teammates.

7 TIMES TO SPEED UP

1. Be quick to dismiss nonperformers and detractors. Don't let them drag you and others down.
2. Be quick to cut projects when they're not living up to expectations, even if you're in the middle of creating the projects, and especially once they're launched and data shows your assumptions were wrong.
3. Be quick to offer *specific* feedback.
4. Be quick to correct your course.

5. Be quick to admit your mistakes.
6. Be quick to promote from within. Empower your associates with the understanding that their hard work, drive, and interests will take them places within your organization. Give them a path with honest feedback and opportunities.
7. Be quick to try. We follow the Silicon Valley mindset of "fail often and fail fast." Instead of wringing your hands and calling multiple meetings, take it one piece at a time and view each piece as a test. Doesn't work? Move on to the next. Worked great? Double down and try to make it better. Hire people who share that mentality.

The more complex the decision, the more time you need to think about it. When you know the direction you're headed, you also know the opportunities that arise that require fast action. More important, with clarity of vision, you more easily reject otherwise great ideas that are inconsistent with that vision. That's one of the hardest things to do. No one likes to cut good ideas, and almost everyone believes they can do more than they think. Best to cut first, then when you complete the first project, add another. Seems so obvious, but it's something we say we will do, but seldom do.

"He's very thoughtful in his approach," Steve said of my decision-making. "He's not reactive. He is calculating in a good way. If it's a hard decision, he is not going to go right at it. He's going to steer, and he's going to influence versus be directive. He's looking at the impact on people. So, therefore, he plays chess constantly."

Working in this way—strategizing what ideas fit into company culture, opening the floor up to every member of the team, and freeing yourself up to focus further into the future with the trust that your executives and associates can handle the day-to-day—allows a leader to continue thinking big. It keeps the entrepreneurial spark alive even through the tasks a CEO must attend to. If you don't think big, experimenting always, then you're not evolving, and that's never good.

GIVING AND TAKING A PUNCH
Maximizing Stakeholder Relationships

I get by with a little help from my friends.
—Ringo Starr

Thinking big works, too, when you're raising money. Unless you have a large Total Addressable Market (TAM), which, among other things, represents the potential revenue for your product or service, and an effective way to tap into it, you'll be hard-pressed to capture anyone's interest. Plus, you need investors to believe you have the ferociousness to capture it.

One of the private equity firms we negotiated with was Highland Capital, with the late Tom Stemberg, the founder of Staples, leading their diligence. Ultimately, Tom said to me, "We think you and Daniel are outstanding entrepreneurs, but you chose the wrong industry."

Ouch. If Tom, a disrupter himself, couldn't see our long-term value, what were we thinking? This was in 2011, three years before we merged with Home Depot.

Highland's business analyst told us the unsatisfying valuation they had modeled, and their willingness to extend a term sheet would be based on that low valuation. We told them not to bother. That seriously deflated our confidence. Tom and team had taken us to the Final Four while they were in Houston, so with that keen attentiveness we expected a sizable offer. I recall within a year after our merger with Home Depot when I was speaking at an investment conference in Boston, where Highland is based, one of their senior partners was told of our exit. He wasn't happy that his firm had essentially passed on our deal. This gave me no joy, though, because it just goes to show that whatever you may think about your own business, others may not have the same opinion. This goes back to my tried and true practice: your best bet is to diversify your approach by simultaneously pursuing many uncorrelated alternatives—as resolutely suggested in Ray Dalio's book *Principles*. So, best to move on.

Move on we did. We raised money from Morgan Stanley Expansion Capital—our first and only institutional capital—and, incredibly, a full sixteen years after launch. Lincoln Isetta and Bobby Bassman, the two principals charged with evaluating and pursuing us and the pair who initially thought our presentation deck was lackluster, came to our office for the first time. As Bobby recalled, "Daniel and Jay took us on a tour. As we walked through The Alley, there was a kickboxing dummy wearing a Home Depot apron. Jay promptly gave it an overhand right to the face. I thought, *I'm going to like this guy*, and, *That's a strong punch!* I hadn't yet learned that Jay had taken boxing lessons for fourteen years."

We'd come to view Home Depot and Lowe's as our main competition—not other online blinds retailers, though there were many. If we could favorably position ourselves (i.e., *anchor*) against big-box stores, as I learned in the book *Positioning: The Battle for Your Mind* by Al Ries and Jack Trout, we believed we could more easily gain market share. Prospective do-it-yourself customers already understood big boxes as the best place to go for low prices and a large assortment. We knew we could do the same, and many times with lower prices. With so little overhead and expertly trained Design Consultants, we were also able to provide true design expertise without charging more.

Once we merged with Home Depot, we could help Home Depot gain that same advantage for its sales of blinds online. Moreover, the economies of scale from combining our purchasing power with that of Home Depot's made buying blinds from both companies a *no-brainer* for customers. And so life came full circle.

Almost two years later, the dummy, which we called "Joe," was still there when Home Depot came for the first time to inspect us. It was very early that morning, and while they were on their way, I noticed Joe was still wearing the Home Depot apron. That wouldn't do. So, we quickly found a T-shirt that was blue, the color of Lowe's, wrote "Lowe's" on it with a thick black marker, and switched it just in time. Knowing what we know now about the fierce competition between Lowe's and Home Depot, that symbol of wanting to bash Lowe's surely resonated with the Home Depot execs.

If I've made it seem so far as if fundraising was easy, it certainly was not, especially when we were targeting the big guys. The difficulty was exacerbated because it distracted us from running our business. The first seven equity funds we approached rejected us. Nothing. I thought maybe it was our approach; turns out, it was. Everything changed after I read Peter Guber's *Tell to Win*, which is about how to tell compelling, purposeful stories in a way that resonates with your particular audience. Beforehand, I had been using just data, metrics, and numbers, which to us seemed quite persuasive. But, after reading Guber's book, I began storytelling, too. The next seven funds all made us offers. The key for us was passionately explaining our long-term vision of moving to adjacent product categories. And a solid overhand right I wasn't afraid to use.

Beware of Pigeons

When you are successful, your people will manage the short term, freeing you up to expand your horizons and scout ahead. For some entrepreneurs, the focus is always on the exit, and there's nothing wrong with that. I prefer to focus on growth, because I don't want an exit to be the only measure of success. And I love growing a business—in fact, even after selling GCC, I stayed over six years focusing on growth. Growth is continuous improvement.

Nevertheless, you shouldn't have complete disregard for the exit. And when you have institutional investors, as we did finally in 2012 with Morgan Stanley, there's an expectation that you're going to sell, usually within five years of the funding. So, we prepared for an exit, even as we focused on growth. Our goal was to maintain our 20–25 percent annual growth rate, even at the sacrifice of profit. But because we knew at some point profit was going to be important in terms of valuation, we made sure our EBITDA (our Earnings Before Interest, Taxes, Depreciation, and Amortization) was no less than 5 percent. We didn't want to decrease our advertising expense at the cost of growth purely to show more profit, so we continued to advertise aggressively. Our board helped us think through this decision, as did talking with investment bankers to get their perspectives on what buyers wanted. Consistent growth was essential, as long as it wasn't coming at the expense of the bottom line and gross profit (essentially the difference between the amount you sell a product for and its cost), we were told. We also created financial models that showed how we could directly control and regulate growth and the resulting profit, so once we were sold, to grow fast or generate profit could be left up to the discretion of the buyer. That was one of the smartest things we ever did. Thank you, board.

In retrospect, it's a good idea no matter what to have a legitimate board.

The first board we created, pre–growth capital, was not ideal, but it got us where we needed to be. It consisted of three acquaintances of mine plus two strategic investors who owned a blinds manufacturing factory in Dallas. That manufacturer was selling us our private label product and they wanted to grow their business. They saw the internet as a chance for them to expand nationally and sell their product through us.

They were my biggest investors early on, and they were very helpful. We developed a supply agreement. I got blinds. I got money. They had a strong relationship with their bank, so when we wanted to buy JustBlinds.com in 2005, they put up their factory as collateral and we used their bank to borrow the money needed to finance the deal. That was an enormous help and much appreciated. One of the two owners frequently reminded me that he also gave me my first computer. At the time I got it, that computer seemed as valuable as his offered collateral.

Later, we discovered that in some ways they were not as helpful as we had initially thought, but we were required to buy from them because of our supply agreement. They were getting it both ways. There was an inherent conflict of interest. They profited from selling us blinds, and they also owned part of our company. So where was their allegiance? To our profitability or theirs? It was almost a parasitic relationship.

I wanted to grow the company, and that meant putting all the profit we made back into it, something neither they, nor any of the other investors, wanted to do. They all wanted cash distributions. We were not in alignment, and no business can grow when it doesn't know in which direction to do so. It was clear then that my optimism for becoming far greater than a blinds retailer did not resonate with the other investors. Their shortsightedness was extremely frustrating, even though I was the one benefiting the most (short term) because I owned the biggest percentage of the company and received the biggest portion of the cash distributions.

One of my investors believed that every idea he sent our way was an AMAZING IDEA! I make use of capitalization here because those emails always used an abundance of capitalized hyperboles, insisting that we urgently employ his VERY SMART ideas. That sort of disruption was something I shielded the team from, with instructions to them that if they were to receive such an email or call, it was to be referred to me for follow-up. That usually resulted in me giving him a call to discuss the idea, or emailing him and *thanking* him for the suggestion.

On the other hand, while it was easy to get conditioned to being bothered by intrusive behavior and to dismiss the idea, occasionally his ideas were actually brilliant. One was a proposed deal term with a financial institution. He vehemently objected to it and I thought he was being overly picky. I relented and was able to negotiate it to his satisfaction. When we sold the company to Home Depot, his idea saved us millions of dollars.

I once heard an expression that investors (and board members) are like pigeons. They fly in, leave a mess, then fly away. That won't happen if you work hard to understand each of your board members' superpowers, their unique points of view, and what they care about. That means you ask, carefully listen—and *hear* them.

But you shouldn't always follow their advice. Your board includes smart and seasoned professionals who are likely more experienced than you, from whom you want and need advice. Yet they will not be privy to the inner dynamics of your business or understand it as well as you and your team, so you'll get frustrated by advice that sometimes seems off base, even illogical.

Many entrepreneurs I know tell me that once they get a company to a certain size where a board becomes integral to decision-making, they're out. Too frustrating, as I was reminded constantly. One particular board member resisted every hire I made, worried I would bloat our overhead. Another time, the board insisted I hire an investment banker to handle the negotiations with Home Depot. This suggestion I ignored. Not only were Daniel and I just fine, especially with the help of our attorney, but I was worried the third-party banker would just approve *any* deal, not the *best* deal, because no deal would mean no fee for the banker. I sometimes wonder how we ever got approvals for our capital budgets for technology, but then realize it all comes down to my practice of learning as I go. We just did it without approvals because we didn't yet know that was something we should have done. (Of course, I know now that it's the board's duty to set such expectations and guidelines, but that's another thing entirely.)

I wish I could tell you there's a trick to making the right decisions when faced with board opposition. As CEO, you have a duty to comply with your board and a duty to do the right thing. The approach I used was learned from years of meditation. Recognize and acknowledge the trap, but don't try to judge it. Then objectively note how you're reacting. "I'm feeling frustrated and anxious. OK." Ask others for advice, then unemotionally go back to the board member and state your case. I've found with board members, when you go one-on-one and they lose the pressure to posture in front of other board members, they almost always do the right thing. Once again, you may be the one who is wrong.

Yes, you give up a lot of control when you have a board, and especially when you take outside money. But the idea, of course, is to mitigate your risk—give up the least amount of control you can. In our supply agreement, we added a buyout clause, suggested by our incredible attorney, Susan Pravda, from Foley & Lardner's Boston office. (Susan is also the attorney who I believed obviated the need for an investment banker.) That allowed us to, at any time, buy them out at a strike price, based on a fixed price. At the time, that price seemed high to everyone, including me. So no one, including the investors, gave it much thought.

"They effectively had a lot of control over us early on," Daniel remembered. "We didn't realize how tightly our hands were tied. The lesson is not to have suppliers be your investors, especially with a strict supply agreement. Though this generally applies whenever a strategic investor has a stake but also benefits from some sort of preferential agreement. Enter into those arrangements with open eyes. Have a way out.

"The process of bringing in money is just grueling and a huge distraction. We interviewed so many firms about a minority investment, and eventually Morgan Stanley did it. But when we were able to kick out these suppliers, it was like magic how much freedom we had. Until then we had naively thought we were getting a good price. But when we could shop around, bingo! Our costs got so much better, as did our flexibility and innovation. And we were able to develop supply chain and merchandising prowess.

"Jay was able to see some of these things way in advance. For example, he had the vision to say we needed to bring in outside money and kick out these suppliers. We were doing fine. Everything was good. But he had a sense we would do better if we could get free. Over the course of about ten years, we doubled our margin by having the freedom to shop around."

So, we took money from Morgan Stanley and made them an owner, then bought out the strategic stockholders (who, yes, were pissed).

Daniel and I flew out to meet them for dinner where we told them the news. I've had more congenial dinners. But we did it, and we were able to put significant money on the balance sheet to grow the company.

Just two years later, we sold the company while not actively trying to do so.

Boards Are Not Boring

In the time between, we built a robust board we felt confident in. Morgan Stanley held two seats, one original investor and I remained, and we agreed to add three more independents that Morgan Stanley and I would jointly determine.

Choosing a board is important, and it was a point of disagreement between Daniel and me at that stage in our growth.

"I had read all this stuff about how you can lose control with your board, so I was pushing him to stack the deck," Daniel said, referring to his suggestion of putting himself and Barbara on the board so we didn't lose control. "Jay said, 'No, we need to have an independent board,'" Daniel remembered. "And he was right because it brought a lot of credibility. And we learned how to make your supply chain a valuable asset."

Make sure you know why you want your board. What purpose will it serve? Are you just looking for marquee names? To raise money? Connections? Are you really trying to build a company of substance?

Marquee names help, but you also require substance that is useful and specific to your business and your needs. We added Todd Krasnow, the former CMO of Staples. We needed to know how to grow, and Todd knew how to do that well. We also added Rick Darling, who ran a $10 billion multinational consumer goods sourcing company. We were looking for sourcing and supply. I needed somebody familiar with distribution and licensing. He was an international expert at it.

Our prospective board members were sourced from strong relationships Morgan Stanley held and from my own research and contacts. Some people Morgan Stanley said would be great as the third independent board member were, on paper, superstars. But I was looking for a particular value, and they weren't able to provide that. So I told Morgan Stanley no. And I held out.

Once you have your board, use it. Don't view it as a necessary evil. If you really want to improve, these should be people who will ask you the tough questions you really should have asked yourself. Once we adopted that mindset, our board made us better. Later, Home Depot made us even better. We learned how to ask ourselves tough questions, and it turned out the most frustrating thing about getting tough questions from others was that we hadn't already thought of them ourselves.

A lot of time goes into preparing for board meetings. Getting every bullet right on your board presentation can be a never-ending task. Version forty-one, anyone? And usually, once you get in the meeting, the questions start, and before you know it, it's time to end the meeting and you're only on page three! The thing to keep in mind is that the preparation you did makes you better because you were able to crystallize the team's thoughts on your recent performance and needed next steps. It's possible that you might not have given your business sufficient analysis had you not prepared for your board.

Earlier-stage companies, as long as they haven't yet taken in investment capital from an institutional fund (because they probably will want a board seat), might be better off with an *advisory board* versus a full board. At that stage, you probably don't need the strict governance of a real board and it's easier to attract advisory board members because their duties are lighter and the legal liability is less.

5 WAYS TO MAXIMIZE YOUR RELATIONSHIPS WITH ADVISORS AND BOARDS

1. Readily seek information from everyone, and ultimately, unless governance restricts your decision, you make the final call.
2. View all input as a gift and not defensively. If you're going to be upset by a question, then be upset by the fact that you didn't think of the question yourself.
3. When answering a question you had already thought of, don't dismiss the question. Instead, acknowledge that it is a good question, one you and your team had considered already, and had even come to a preliminary conclusion similar to the one implied by the questioner, but after more careful review of specific or possibly new facts, you concluded otherwise. Be respectful and candid.
4. Ensure your advisors are true experts in categories relevant to your growth trajectory.
5. Be aware that it's acceptable to weigh some people's opinions more than others, though also know that sometimes those with the least amount of experience come up with the most obvious solutions, because of that lack of experience.

THE ORANGE BLOSSOM TRAIL

Proven Lessons to Overcome the
Poor Odds of a Successful Merger

The purpose of relationships is not to have another complete you.
But to have another with whom to share your completeness.
—Neale Donald Walsch

Going through the process of selling the company was heady and surreal. And yes, this is finally the moment where I'm going to detail the process of how this all happened for GCC and Home Depot. While it was everything we could have hoped for, it was terrifying, too, and I dealt with the stress of it all by focusing on the assumption that it was not going to happen.

We kept it very quiet, using the code name "Sunrise." Only my C-suite knew what was going on. Almost every meeting with Home Depot was just Daniel and me, sitting in a big room with any number of executives from Home Depot. We never created an investment pitch book. And, as previously referenced, we never hired an investment banker.

Lots of experience with potential investors and buyers had taught us to never bet that a deal was going to happen. That mentality would only ever distract us too much or, worse, drive our behavior, making us overly cocky and shortsighted.

Some companies start to game numbers at this phase so they're super-positioned for a sale. They spend less (or more) on advertising than normal, cut labor costs, new benefits, and so on. In the short term, when talks are going well with the potential buyer, those window-dressing ideas seem brilliant. But what happens if the sale doesn't go through? You're screwed!

So we just operated the company per usual. To Home Depot and others who were interested, we just presented our existing operating monthly or quarterly reports. By not creating a special presentation deck, and by maintaining business as usual, we telegraphed to potential suitors that, while we wanted a deal, if it didn't happen, we'd be no worse for wear. And that was true. The truly interested parties would note the investment capital we'd taken just two years before from Morgan Stanley Expansion Capital, however, and understand inherently that we were very open to talking.

In fact, it was our relationship with Morgan Stanley that made us even more attractive to Home Depot. Sami Nassar, their director of strategic business development at the time, said, "We knew that Morgan Stanley did more diligence prior than we would probably do," explaining that our recent relationship with Morgan Stanley implied our fitness and trustworthiness as a company.

We took ourselves seriously. We'd leveraged Morgan Stanley's relationships and hired Ernst & Young and Silicon Valley Bank—both commonly used by high-growth, entrepreneurial companies—to make sure there was nothing amiss in our finances. We had a legitimate board and proper governance, and we'd previously begun having our financial statements audited just for such an occasion, years before there was any real interest on the horizon. I learned this lesson—namely, to run a company as if it were already a public company—from a successful Houston entrepreneur and businessman whom I've always admired, Doug Erwin. Doug had been the chief operating officer of BMC Software and CEO of several companies with big financial exits. He went on to lead his own company helping entrepreneurs, and his advice proved invaluable. Harken back to my advice about seeing your future needs and minding the gaps today.

As a result of those moves, Home Depot thought we'd been positioning ourselves to go public, and while that had occurred to us, we knew we weren't quite ready for that. We didn't think GCC would be perceived at its full potential for at least another couple of years, so while going public was a possibility on the horizon, it was not something we were angling for just yet. This turned out to be a good thing anyway, because acquiring companies want to know there's a lot of upside after they buy you, and showing potential growth and future revenue is a big bonus to acquirers . . . just don't expect to be paid upfront for that future growth and upside.

So, the whole time, we went on operating at GCC as if nothing were changing in terms of ownership. We continued to expand; we continued to advertise. We went forward creating our singular road map for the next five years, as if there were no purchase offer already signed, showcasing that potential for future growth as we did so.

While that was strategically smart—again, deals fall through all the time—it was also very much about my personal state of mind. Although we had a contract to sell, I never hired any personal wealth advisors. I never thought about what I was going to do with my money. I set up no bank accounts, nothing. I didn't want to be depressed at the thought of what could have been if it ended up not happening. Further, if I had already envisioned the money as mine before a sale went through, I might agree to request late-breaking contract terms to prevent *losing* that money before it was *actually* mine. I also tried not to think about what I might do with the proceeds from the sale; certainly never spoke aloud about it. That way, the worst that could happen was we still had a company that was profitable and growing at 20 percent every year. Not a bad outcome.

That was the enviable position we were in when we got the call from Mike Mahler, who, at the time, was Home Depot's Merchandising Vice President of the Blinds department, among other products. "You guys want to have a meeting?" he asked.

We said, "Sure. Why not?"

Our board advised us not to offer much information in that first meeting because Home Depot could have been just fishing. So we gave accurate information, but didn't provide any specific financials. When they asked us about profitability, we said it was "better than Amazon" and "you'll be surprised." I like to use the expression "you'll be surprised."

And they were surprised. We were still growing at 20 percent, plus we were profitable. Our gross margin was exceptionally good and had been growing every year for four or five years, and not just by a little, but by over 400 basis points. We were first in our category online, by far.

That fact didn't matter at first to Home Depot, though. As I've touched on already, at that stage they were just looking to buy technology—an online *configurator* that could price the infinite number of blinds configurations among the different types, fabrics, colors, sizes, and upgrade options. But during his hunt to find the right prospect, Sami asked himself an especially important question. As a leader, there are many times when you need to stop, clear your mind, and ask yourself, "What am I really trying to do?"

While Sami had been given the green light to find and purchase a configurator technology to increase Home Depot's blinds sales online, the real goal wasn't even the technology; it was the revenue that technology would bring in for them.

"If you're trying to corner the market and be a destination for all things window coverings, including online, it's a much bigger play," Sami said, adding, "What do you want the headline to be: 'Home Depot buys dinky technology,' or 'Number one home improvement retailer buys number one online window coverings retailer'?" I like Sami.

I found out later that Home Depot had almost purchased a different small company whose platform was nowhere near as versatile or powerful or scalable as ours. But then Mike suggested they talk to the number one player, us, and they were quite taken.

The 35-Minute Meatloaf Lunch

"I remember taking a trip down to Houston to visit his team," said Home Depot's then online president Kevin Hofmann. "You're looking for the health of the business, the capabilities of the team, the culture, you're looking for some congruence around mutual goals and objectives. You're basically on a first date.

"I loved it right from the start," Kevin said of our first meeting. "Jay had created a culture and a vibe of togetherness, of caring concern for the associates, for entrepreneurialism and continuous growth."

In essence: it was our core values that sealed the deal for us, despite the competition.

"For all kinds of companies, there's the culture and the value set that's on the website and in the blog post and on the laminated card connected to employee badges," Kevin said. "There's the intention, but very rarely does what's on the laminated card actually get put into practice. What I always appreciated about Jay, and it was evident within the first couple of meetings, is the guy really believes in it passionately.

"He wakes up every morning thinking about how to live his values and his cultural vibe. And he constantly evangelizes it. His cultural values and ideals permeated all levels of the organization, and it didn't hurt that a lot of his cultural values were congruent to what we were trying to stand for at Home Depot."

Once Kevin and the leadership team decided we were the right ones to match their needs, they had to convince the CEO, Frank Blake.

"We thought we had a pretty compelling story," Kevin remembered. "It would really help our blinds business. We thought we'd also have options to grow into other categories. We had a great big PowerPoint prepared for it.

"And important to note: we hadn't done a lot of acquisitions. I think there'd been five or six over the past five or six years, and I had done most of them. It's very hard to get this stuff done inside large companies."

When they finally secured a meeting with Frank to present their idea to acquire us, I'm told it was a clear done deal from the start.

"We were up in a dining room inside the Home Depot headquarters, and, of all things, we had a meatloaf lunch," Kevin said. "And it was a fast lunch. We didn't even look at the PowerPoint. I never told Jay this, but we worked on this idea for two or three months leading up to our meeting with him. Then we probably courted Jay for another month after that, but in the end, we decided to do it over a thirty-five-minute meatloaf lunch."

A Match Made in Orange

Throughout the whole process, Home Depot was very transparent and candid, which is why we had a great relationship from the start. They wanted to buy. They made us an offer. We haggled, certainly, but came to an agreement pretty quickly, although the board and I differed on what was an acceptable offer. Despite my belief that the original offer was fair, the board rejected it outright. Easy for them to say! My life was on the line. My family's finances were at stake.

So, I went back to Home Depot, which turned out to be a good thing. We got more. I confidently told the board the new offer, but they were still not satisfied. I was dumbfounded. *You've got to be kidding,* I grumbled. I went back to Home Depot again. This time I was stonewalled. Thankfully, the board acquiesced, and we came to terms. I was nervous the whole time, thinking I was going to blow the deal. Each day of those negotiations were the peak of my anxiety. Remember my 1–10 having-a-great-day scale? I was definitely at a 2 each time.

Home Depot's first offer came verbally from their acquisition lead analyst, George Mattingly, after doing much high-level diligence. I was at a small conference near Austin, Texas, at the time, where none other than Frank Blake, Home Depot's CEO, was speaking about Conscious Capitalism. I was told not to approach him, and he was told not to approach me. It was a coincidence, but maybe not. Was it fate?

Immediately after Frank's talk, there was a break and I was standing outside relaxing. Then I got the call. "Jay, we're prepared to make you an offer," George said. Prior to that moment, there'd been no guarantee an offer was going to be made. None. So George's affirmative phrase caused me to start shaking. After I heard the amount, I continued to shake for several minutes. Overcome with emotion, my eyes began to water. I stood there outside, stunned. I called my wife and told her, and no one else. Barbara had been with me for much of my journey with GCC and she deserved to be the first to know. The board could wait. Morgan Stanley could wait. My team could wait. Then I walked back into the conference, and Frank was gone.

The detailed diligence was done just a few months after that. Of course, since we'd been running the company as if we might go public, without the Sarbanes-Oxley type of requirements, our records were accessible and organized. Whatever was requested was furnished swiftly.

After the negotiation was over, but just three weeks before we were scheduled to close, George and Sami noticed that our sales dipped slightly. It was a seasonal dip, so it was nothing out of the ordinary, but I was driving one evening to a charity event, and on the way, I got a call from George telling me they were flying in the next morning.

What?!

I knew that there was a clause in our buying agreement—as there is in most buying agreements—that gave Home Depot an out for a material adverse change (MAC clause), but I hadn't thought that our very normal, very weatherable yearly dip was going to trigger it. I was haunted that night, unable to sleep, not knowing what they might be thinking. The next day, George and Sami showed up and expressed concern over our flat forecast for January.

"You go on a twenty-plus run rate, then drop to flat, yeah, there was a little bit of freak-out," Sami recalled.

We explained to them a revenue drop from December to January was common for us, and that year over year, we were still demonstrating strong growth. Thankfully, this was true and we had historical sales records to prove it. After further review, the merger moved forward.

You Don't Have to Be a Jerk

Nothing is simple. Success stories are replete with such issues. Even today, more than six years after that phone call and unexpected visit, my heartbeat elevated just writing about it. What people don't realize is that no matter how in control and successful one looks from the outside, you just don't have an idea, build it, then sell without a lot of anguish.

In the end, it was kind of a shock that it happened, even more so after the fact when I was given the opportunity to see from the inside of Home Depot how difficult it was to gain consensus and support for capital allocations. That day, though, we celebrated by drinking thirty-year-old Macallan scotch, which was a gift from Barbara, who has always been thoughtful and takes great care in thinking about others, so she knows how to give gifts. I'll never forget that moment. It was January 23, 2014, at 11:28 a.m. when my attorney, Susan Pravda, texted me the image of the Certificate of Merger. That was it. It was done. So then was half the bottle.

It was definitely one of the highlights of my career, especially recounting that it was not so much a company that I'd built, but that I'd put together the *team* that built it. Home Depot could have gotten technology from many places (albeit ours *was* the best), but they could only have gotten the kind of team built on our 4 principles from GCC, and that ended up being just as much of a benefit for them. Whenever I'm asked about my greatest professional accomplishment, the answer is always, "the team." And it took a lot of work to get there, which is in and of itself part of the value. That's the norm for truly successful entrepreneurs—not the flashy images shown in glossy magazines of overnight billionaires. Most companies that succeed take years to get there.

In fact, I believe my experience with GCC, tracking its progress back as far as those first days in Laura's, influences how my children see the scope of their own lives. The media often celebrates people who make it big in a matter of a few years, especially in the tech startup scene, so we're all tricked into believing that's the way to do it. Knowing I was in my late fifties before I finally reached the point where I became successful, at least as externally defined, seems to have given them a bit more patience and a bit less anxiety than some of their peers, because their peers' perception of success is people with really nice sports cars on Instagram.

Just days after the sale, I received a seven-page, handwritten letter from Morgan Stanley's Bobby Bassman. He reminisced about our first meeting and the impression I had made: "passionate, with a bold vision," but with a "PowerPoint deck that [sure] could be improved!"

"You will be congratulated by many on the sale," Bobby wrote. "Hey, it's a spectacular outcome that will make global headlines.

"I'd like to congratulate you . . . for a different reason. I'd like to commend your character, your core principles and values, and the way in which you treat others—from the janitor to the CEO. It is those characteristics that I learned the most during our time together."

When you are at your highest and lowest in life, the type of people you will want around you will be there if you have earned them. That happens by being kind and honest. That's what stuck with Bobby and why we were able to work together so well and help each other grow. You don't have to be a jerk to lead. Paul Graham wrote an insightful essay on the topic, entitled "Why It's Safe for Founders to Be Nice," which I recommend.

What a relief—*human* entrepreneurs really exist.

GCC, Meet Home Depot

I'd had my moment of personal celebration—and personal relief. Now it was time to let the whole team in on the news. The big announcement was made at a SayJay. In order to make sure everyone was there, we did make some additional fanfare that there was going to be a big announcement.

We'd done a terrific job keeping our secret, so when I dropped the news about our sale to Home Depot, it came as a complete shock to most in the room. The only people who knew beforehand were at the very top of the organization: Daniel, Larry, Houston Lane (CFO), Marilynne (Director of Accounting), and Steve Riddell (Chief Sales Officer), who kicked off what was our largest SayJay ever.

After noting that our company was at a crossroads, Steve called me and the senior leadership team to the front of the room. They sat, and I stood as I made perhaps the biggest announcement of my life.

"Today is the beginning of infinity," I said. "Today is a day that has potential beyond anything we've ever thought of before—unlimited opportunity for the company and the blinds industry. But most importantly, the opportunity is for you, my teammates. This could literally turbocharge your career."

Then I made everyone put away any cameras or recording devices. The announcement was still an hour away from being made publicly, and it was vital that the news not leave the room. I trusted all 175 associates to abide by that request, and because of my "walking around" methods over the years, I knew them all well enough to know they would not break my trust.

My kids, Barbara, and Barbara's two adult children, Jenny and Ted, were there, right in the front row. I thanked them first, becoming openly emotional, which is a normal tendency of mine. Then I thanked my family who had left us—Naomi and my parents.

I thanked our original investors, all of them, by name. I thanked the Morgan Stanley leaders who invested in us, all of them, by name, too. I thanked our board of directors by name. I also thanked our advisors.

Then I finally let the bright orange cat out of the Home Depot bag.

"I am proud to announce, with optimism and confidence, respect and admiration for everything you've done, the merger of the number one blinds company in the world, Global Custom Commerce, and the number one home improvement retailer in the world, The Home Depot."

The room erupted in instant applause that went on for almost a minute and ended with a standing ovation of our entire staff. Their reaction was one of the most generous things I'd witnessed as CEO. Everyone knew how much a deal like that would mean to me, what a success it would be to have a giant of industry want what we had built. The operative word there is *we*. That applause and support was for me and for our business, yes, but in reality, it was for themselves. They'd done it without having the slightest idea what this merger would mean for them individually. So, my first responsibility was to reassure them and answer those unspoken, but obvious questions—which is, as you'll remember, how I've always broken big news.

"I know what you're thinking. What's going to change? First of all, the walls are not going to be painted orange," I joked.

"Second of all, in every Home Depot store, there's going to be an Alley."

Silence ensued as everyone contemplated what that might look like—because, yes, that seemed totally feasible and believable. I had been kidding, of course, and hadn't expected that earnest reaction, but in retrospect we'd done so many far-fetched things before, so *why not?*

"Everybody keeps their job."

I repeated that three times.

"This deal was done because they want *you*. They want what *we* created, which they could not do on their own, so they bought it. Compensation, benefits go up," I continued, again to applause. "What about the culture? They love the culture here. They do not want to change it. They don't want to screw up the culture. The culture stays."

I acknowledged there would be changes, primarily to processes. Then I stated very clearly and very firmly, "I am staying."

Thankfully, they applauded again.

"If you thought I was having fun now, how could I possibly pass this up?" I said. "I am not leaving. I don't want to retire, not yet."

Cue the Dysfunction

Of course, even the most perfect of marriages have their issues. The honeymoon period was blissful, but short. There were decisions to be made and transitions to get rolling. The most noticeable first challenge was the immediate effect the merger had on my leadership team. Who is their boss now? What is their role? Will they get recognized? What do their new bosses really care about? Would they be fired? Would they move up?

With me, they'd known what to expect. They knew the qualities I was looking for and how they would be rewarded. Although I assured them little had changed in the management of GCC, there was no hiding the giant orange elephant that appeared in the room at nearly every meeting early on after the merger.

Just as uncertainty will kill a business, the fear of the unknown will eat away at your culture. Unanswered questions or answers they didn't accept prompted bad behavior among my leadership team. During presentations, they would strive to shine independently instead of focusing on the team. When problems arose, some blamed other senior leadership, in essence throwing them under the bus. One by one, senior leaders blamed each other in an effort—driven by fear—to cover their asses, which is never productive. Like a parade of bad behavior, each would come into my office to criticize and diminish a colleague.

Remember that GCC truly felt like a family—a cultural feat I do not take lightly or speak of facetiously. To me, this behavior was on par with turning on a sibling to make yourself look better—something we might expect of a preteen but certainly not an adult member of our senior leadership team. It was painful and unexpected, but really, it was totally logical behavior following such a big change in our organization. But it was the first time it had happened to us and it went on for many months.

I repeatedly told the leaders to work it out between themselves, trying to avoid making them always dependent on me to resolve their differences. It didn't work, so I turned to my tried and true practice of just-in-time learning. One book came to the rescue: Patrick Lencioni's *Silos, Politics and Turf Wars: A Leadership Fable About Destroying the Barriers That Turn Colleagues into Competitors*.

The book advises establishing a North Star for everyone to rally around. It could be a common enemy or a common mission, where everybody has certain roles in achieving that mission. For us, that became our 2020 Vision—the brochures and the Billion Brainer Tower dream (see how it's all coming together?). Suffice it to say, this was a grand enough project that everyone could rally behind it: there was a timeline, there were metrics on how we were going to judge ourselves, and everyone had clearly defined and separate roles and responsibilities. For the benefit of the team, mine was to influence the leadership of Home Depot around The 2020 Vision and start to acclimate them to the idea that we were more than a blinds company.

Not only did it work to bring everyone together and remind us of the team we needed to be, but we also actually created something meaningful and important to our entire company and our journey. The 2020 Vision became more than a North Star; it became our universe.

Even with your leadership team on the same page and working in harmony, it's not easy to create change within a hundred-billion-dollar company, especially change that requires the creation of new technology, new processes, or a compensation policy inconsistent with their norm, all of which were the case for us. We came with too many existing priorities and established policies, and, really, we were just a small fish in HD's big pond.

Compensation was an especially thorny issue for us. Our Customer Engagement Center is another ingredient of our secret sauce. Highly trained, routinely coached and mentored, with quality ensured, these associates (who handle sales, customer care, chat, social media, and emails) are compensated in a unique way. We pay them royally when they give exceptional service and value, and virtually nothing when they don't. This is called Performance-Based Compensation (PBC), and it was originally formulated by Steve Riddell, whose background excels in maximizing performance of contact centers. Over time, Steve's system has been tweaked by our analysts and leaders to provide just the right balance of increased performance that customers notice and labor costs that decrease as they scale (leverage). It is a marvel, even though, as is true of all compensation programs, it can be gamed, causing associates' behaviors to be not in the best interests of other associates or the business.

The compensation system's brilliance is that it does not pay strictly on sales and quantity of interactions. It also pays based on quality. Our internal quality assurance team listens to calls and grades them on such things as, "Was the right solution suggested? Was the customer treated kindly and with respect? Was the customer delighted by the interaction?" This type of program, where pay is not fixed but varies by some formula, is called *variable compensation.*

However, we were informed that variable compensation was generally inconsistent with Home Depot's practices, so we were asked to change it. Well, it was obviously a time to **Express Ourselves**. And express we did, explaining the benefits to a series of executives, and going up the long ladder of executives to garner needed approvals to win the battle. Multiple meetings. Multiple decks. Much time.

Since it was so soon after the merger, and no one had mentioned it beforehand, this pushback was a shock to our system. In the end, as with most things when properly explained, Home Depot honored one of *their* eight core values: *Do the Right Thing*. We were allowed to keep our highly effective compensation system, but the fact that this critical piece of our success was questioned solely because it was inconsistent with Home Depot's policies raised many of GCC's associates' antennas that we might have gotten ourselves into something we weren't prepared for, further exacerbating tension among the troops.

Since then, however, execs throughout the Home Depot enterprise have visited us to learn how they might apply variable compensation to their teams, and how they might otherwise learn about how we operate.

Such was the case in 2018 when we first launched the Measure & Install (M&I) program, which was taking us back into customers' homes for the first time since the Laura's days. GCC had already captured the lion's share of the DIY blinds market online. But online DIY is still a limited group—only about 8 percent of at least a $5 billion market. The preponderance of sales come not from people doing it themselves or online, but from having people do it for them (DIFM).

No prioritization to partner with us was built into other Home Depot divisions, so we did what we'd always done: we just started. We built our own technology and an app for the service associates who would be going into people's homes. We blended the online and in-home blinds markets, using our CEC to assist the service providers who were measuring and installing. They uploaded the measurements, which instantly synced into the customer's account with GCC.

For the first time, a customer could complete an entire Product + Service purchase online. And, lo and behold, instead of selling an "idea" to the corporate machine, we were selling a real solution and a plan. Guess what? That's a lot easier, and it worked. We're now in almost the entire country with M&I and, because we've proven it out, our model will integrate into the stores. That's a big win for Home Depot customers. I recall when selling my Laura's Drapery store decades earlier, I swore I never wanted to have another physical store, and now I had over 2000. See, I can evolve.

Large companies are less prone to take risks—to experiment without fear of failure—because so much is at stake. When you have a novel untested idea, it's sometimes best to save your breath and frustration—don't waste your time trying to convince others to do it. Instead, do it in stealth mode. Don't spend a lot of money, work out the bugs, and then unveil your results.

"It was a perfect example of how the whole business rallied," said Steve O'Connor. "The team was working nights and weekends to get it done, so we could start taking market share."

The successful execution of a new idea often requires other people's help, especially when it's a big idea. To engage others in an idea that remains locked in your brain is a leader's challenge. You must be able to create a clear and inspiring vision—something your team so fully buys into that they become vested in the successful outcome. That's why our team worked so tirelessly to launch M&I. Not because we told them they had to, but because they were excited to prove they could do something new and consequential. Everyone wants to feel they're consequential.

Welcome to the New Reality

As unique and critical as our culture is, any merger or acquisition was going to cause disruption, and that has been a challenging part of our journey. Fortunately, Home Depot was aware they sometimes had communication and operational challenges with their acquisitions. They were sensitive about not diluting our potential long-term value, which I appreciated. However, there's no getting around the fact that connecting our independent operation to a mothership the size of Home Depot was going to change things.

"It was a massive cultural difference," Daniel said. "It was like putting a goldfish into a bag of warm water to help it adapt to the cold water over time. And Jay did a good job of that. He saw his job as very much about keeping the walls from closing in. Home Depot had the inertia of an elephant—as good natured and as good intentioned as they were, it couldn't be stopped. One of the things we could have done better is well-defined modes of interaction, and over time, we did it. But initially, anyone in Atlanta could call anyone in Houston and it wasn't clear who had authority to make demands from us. They were killing us with attention.

"The reason for that is Home Depot had seldom bought companies, and some of the ones they did buy did not live up to expectations," Daniel added. "Well, Jay was constantly reminding them to keep them out of our business and keep our bubble intact. The downside, though, is that we were supposed to be this influencer inside of Home Depot and change the way they sell, and you can't do that if you're trying to separate yourselves. So there was a delicate balance between staying autonomous and at the same time getting involved in all kinds of their stuff."

Our senior leadership team felt it first when the relationship became imbalanced, which continued to happen occasionally over the years, requiring recalibration. One of the first examples of needing to shift our boundaries came closely after the merger, with what Home Depot calls a *merchant*, or someone of high responsibility who handles the pricing, merchandising, and many other objectives for a class/subclass of products.

"He started to tell us whom we could hire and how much we could pay—really micromanaging us like we were a new toy he'd been given," said Daniel. "A few other people and I said, 'We can't take any more, Jay. He's trying to run our business from there.' It was just way too intrusive. Jay likes a fight."

I do have that reputation, perhaps because of my years of boxing, but it would be more accurate to say I like a challenge, and my persistence will not wane if I know what needs to be done. My conviction that our autonomy was integral to our value to Home Depot, that it was in the best interests of GCC, Home Depot, and our customers, moved me to take action in this situation. Culture is critical. Values are critical. If we were going to integrate and truly work—and flourish—with Home Depot, I needed to understand the values, culture, and purpose of Home Depot. What better way to do that than to meet with one of its founders, the heart and soul of Home Depot?

To truly understand the foundational core of Home Depot, I needed to meet the legend, Bernie Marcus, one of Home Depot's founders. I reached out for a meeting and traveled to Home Depot headquarters in Atlanta to have breakfast with him in a small conference room. I asked him lots of questions, and we spoke about culture. His reputation as being generous and forthright was spot on. Here was *the* Bernie Marcus speaking with me and Barbara, who was invited to join us. It was a highlight of my time at Home Depot.

In addition to helping me understand his core values, our open conversation gave him the freedom to ask me questions as well, such as, "Hey, Jay, I hear your Blinds.com radio ads are making fun of big-box stores. Why are you doing that?" The next week, we stopped those ads.

Of course, what it also did was tell people at Home Depot that I would go right to the top at any time. The fact that I met with Bernie without getting anyone's prior approval (though I did tell all key executives about it once the meeting was set) made it clear from the very beginning that I would speak my mind respectfully to whomever with no fear. As a leader, that's your job—protect your culture, protect your values, protect your people, fearlessly, respectfully, immediately. This was a perfect time to employ one of our core values, **Express Yourself**.

As part of that conviction and because of my core value of **Evolve Continuously**, I created a presentation for Home Depot on the lessons learned from the acquisition and what might have helped it go more smoothly. I gave it to the executive leader of HR and head of Strategy. I fully realized the nerve that took, telling them they could have done a better job, but my intention was to help them in the future, because they acknowledged they needed help post-acquisition.

"He's always looking for the best answer," noted Larry Hack, our first Chief Technology Officer. "Jay would always say, 'The best answer wins. It doesn't matter where you sit in the organization—the best idea wins.' When we were acquired by Home Depot, he took that same attitude, speaking very openly and having discussions with very senior people at Home Depot. And I think he was perceived as a troublemaker for a while."

The points I made to the strategic business development group regarding merging companies were warmly greeted. Leadership was anxious to hear what I had to say because they recognized they had a problem.

The issues stem from every department trying to optimize immediately and simultaneously after an acquisition. Bernie told me, "The trouble is always that everyone has their own single number to optimize." They were only optimizing their single link in the chain, instead of optimizing the whole chain. We understood why. That's what they were incentivized to do. Merging businesses successfully takes a lot of time.

When you sell a business, you have to take in a lot of information, have a lot of meetings, meet lots of people, and, often, travel to do it—all while you're still running a business. There must be a period to let the acquired company breathe and come up for air. Welcome it to this new world, and make sure the leadership of the acquired company is involved in the strategic planning around its future, with a reasonable time frame for accomplishing it.

Ultimately, I advised Home Depot to have the patience to allow newly acquired businesses to change. When Pixar and Disney merged, as related in the particularly insightful book that includes a section on merging cultures, *Creativity Inc.*, author Ed Catmull, Pixar's CEO, insisted on creating a list of conditions that would help each company understand the benefits the other brought to the merger. The list included where the office would be located, how people would be paid, how decisions would be made—anything that would establish autonomy where it made sense, and integration when that made sense. That was a good lesson for us, and helped us come up with our own list, which included how our variable compensation program, integral to incentivize and hold people accountable, was necessary.

The friction comes when a large company strives to ensure consistency throughout the company. Identical rules can be anathema to success.

While I had suggestions for improvement, everyone still considers our integration a success.

"You have to have sponsorship within the company, and Jay did this so well. He had a sponsor in me, he had a sponsor in Mike Mahler. But he didn't rest there. He made sure he had at least the likability factor and the respect of other key leaders, like Frank Blake. He worked hard to make sure he had a sponsorship flag planted with a few different parties," Kevin said. "That helps protect against what is absolutely going to come: the dreaded organizational changes. The entrepreneur or small company probably doesn't anticipate what happens daily in a big company—chairs moving and people changing roles."

It's true. Over the six years after the merger, I reported to at least five different people. Company leadership changed at nearly every level, including the CEO, who changed within our first year. Each of those instances could have meant hitting the reset button for us to explain our value, our vision, and our strategy. We did ensure that each new boss was indoctrinated in our culture, history, rules of engagement, and how we thought.

"For an entrepreneur thinking about joining a big company, know that whoever's looking you in the eye and shaking your hand is probably thinking about their next job or their next promotion that's going to happen in six months, and they're going to be halfway across the country in a different role," Kevin said.

That constant changing of the guard, in addition to the inertia of big business, can be exhausting. It's another area where my grit has served me well.

"Don't underestimate the need to have resilience around bureaucracy," Kevin said. "Jay never quit. He never gave up. When we talked about new categories, he probably had to pitch that thirty times. To get the centralized IT team to do something for him, he probably had to talk to them fifty times to get something done. They're used to working on $100 billion problems, and here's this guy from Houston that's got this little $100-million-dollar company and he wants us to reprioritize our workload for him.

"The entrepreneur should not underestimate the calorie burn around communicating and lobbying in a big company," he added. "That's why most people want to be an entrepreneur, because they get so damn frustrated with the energy it takes to get decisions and actions out of big institutions."

A Sweet-Smelling Skunk

I first broached the conversation about finding ways for GCC to operate separately from Home Depot with Seth Todd, whom of course I'd recruited away from Home Depot years prior—he'd already downsized from managing thousands of people to managing just forty, and this idea of mine would shrink that number further, down to three devoted solely to innovating. Launching our skunkworks division was part of our 2020 Vision, an iteration of thinking big by making the core business smaller and sectioning off part of the company. Our merger with Home Depot would not be an exit from **Evolving Continuously** or **Experimenting Without Fear of Failure**, but rather a jumping-off point to allow us to do bigger and better things.

Here's how Seth described this innovative model: "Steve O'Connor's team owns the entire core business—anything that's in production, anything that makes money, day-to-day operations. My team owns all the new business development and all the new product development—R&D for Home Depot or developing Jay's crazy ideas or my crazy ideas. The things we're trying to do are things that no one else anywhere in retail does. And we want to be the first ones to do it, through Home Depot. We want to change the world and the way retail works."

I can hear my original vision clearly in Seth's description, even years later, which means I was successful in articulating it. Like most of my ideas, it was not original. It came to me reading the book *Dual Transformation: How to Reposition Today's Business While Creating the Future* by Scott D. Anthony, Clark G. Gilbert, and Mark W. Johnson. The organizational structure is also sometimes referred to as an *ambidextrous organization*. That term resonated with our team and it stuck. The clarity of bifurcating our business also enabled us to divide out our income statement, budget, and capital allocation. The importance of this cannot be overstated because making Plan (also referred to as *hitting your numbers*) is the single most important thing you must do. It's table stakes. When you don't make Plan, you don't earn the right to do anything else. When people ask my advice for the key objectives for a company that's just sold, my first advice is: make Plan. My second: make Plan.

If the goal, then, is to hit your numbers, doing experimental things is counterproductive because most experiments do not work. If all your experiments work, or most of them do, they're almost certainly *not* experiments. Don't kid yourself; if you're sure that an initiative is going to work, you're not experimenting. Watch for that fallacy in your direct reports because they want to look good in front of you, so the tendency is to be safe. Safe is fine. Just don't pretend they're experiments. If you want to see your folks experiment, you must create a safe space for them to do so. We'd always touted experimentation, and there was no way I was going to let that change just because we were now part of a bigger company.

The inefficiency of experimentation is anathema to making Plan, which is one of the reasons many people in big organizations do *not* feel comfortable **Experimenting Without Fear of Failure**. They very much fear failure. They fear getting fired. Here, the upside of an enormously successful experiment is more than counterbalanced (i.e., negative asymmetry) by the possibility of getting fired, or at the very least hurting their career.

It's exceedingly difficult to innovate when your entire focus is on making Plan. Home Depot's Canadian division was feeling this pain point about the time we merged with them. They were worried about becoming stagnant. They were also worried about stiff competition from Amazon, Lowe's, and Canadian retailer Rona, which Lowe's purchased in 2016.

GCC and Home Depot Canada shared some unique similarities. Like us, Canada was a separate organization from the mothership, using separate technology and enjoying a separate culture and its own operating environment. They also shared our subsidiary stance: take advantage of all the things Home Depot had, but maintain some autonomy and independence. Because of our success, they felt we might be able to offer some guidance. At Home Depot's prompting, some of their leadership team came to Houston to learn how GCC was both disruptive and financially successful at the same time.

After a few meetings, they decided our message was one their entire team needed to hear, so I was invited to come to Canada and speak at one of their strategic planning sessions, which had all their leadership, about one hundred people. I was the keynote speaker for the session.

I was scheduled to arrive the night before to have dinner with some of their folks and Steve O'Connor, who's Canadian himself. I arrived at the Houston airport with plenty of time to spare, but a snowstorm in Canada prevented me from leaving. Back to my home I went, and scheduled a flight early the next morning, requiring me to awaken at 3:30 a.m. When I arrived in Toronto, Steve was there to greet me, having spent the weekend with his family. We took the UP train to downtown Toronto and walked through the snow to the Royal York Hotel. A few hours later, I was onstage with a theme that smacked them in the face.

In my typical nature, I did not beat around the bush. The opening slide of my deck spelled out my thoughts on maintaining an experimental culture: Is Plan Evil?

Presentation to The Home Depot Canadian Division

Most Plans are designed in a way that discourages, if not outright penalizes, growth. For example, let's say you're launching a new product or service, budgeted in the second half of your annual Plan. But you're already ahead of schedule, so you launch it in the first half and it does really well. That seems like the best possible business case. You have something successful, and you can move on to tackling other projects sooner.

However, against Plan, you get a *success penalty* because you grew so fast in the first half of the year, you'll have to undergo what's called a *Re-plan* for the second half. That means whatever Plan you thought you had, it's now been raised. Congrats!

Even if you avoid a Re-plan, most Plans are designed in a way that encourages incremental growth, 3–5 percent annually. If you beat Plan by too much, there isn't typically a lot of compensation incentive and you set a higher hurdle for yourself to make Plan the following year.

However, to miss Plan can be deadly. You are not only severely punished in your remuneration, but it also diminishes your prestige, which limits your ability to continue getting capital and ultimately maintaining your job. You must make Plan.

In other words, I was telling them they had to make Plan, but striving to make Plan would inhibit their ability to innovate, which was their goal. Hence, Plan is evil . . . but there *is* another way.

I got approval from Home Depot's Canadian president and CFO to share this bombastic statement, because they knew I had a workaround—I wasn't stirring a subsidiary revolt. We needed to break out of the idea that Plan is all there is to make. Plan is necessary, yes, but you also need to experiment, and if that doesn't work in a Plan environment, move the experiments out of your normal operating structure.

We separated our experiments, which all had tremendous upside potential, from the iterative and incremental operation of our core business, thereby avoiding negative impact to our income statement by the costs of these experiments. It did take us three years to figure that out, making those first three years a constant struggle of trying to educate the finance team at Home Depot in our methods, as well as those to whom we reported. Educating is a never-ending necessity requiring vigilance. Nonetheless, we never quit because we knew our vision was so compelling, such a part of our DNA and mission, that relinquishing that dream was essentially giving up.

Nope. Not gonna happen.

I flew back to Houston and, after twenty-two hours, my head hit the pillow.

No, Please Not Again

Sometimes things go well and you can get on a Canadian stage and educate a large corporation on how the small guys do some things better. But other times, a decision isn't entirely yours to make, especially when you've handed over the keys to your company. When decisions are made that conflict with what you know is in everyone's long-term best interest, you must comply, but you should also continue doing those things that will eventually cause others to see the light. At those times, my philosophy has been to do the right thing to achieve our mission and ask for forgiveness afterward.

When we merged with Home Depot, they used the name Blinds .com instead of our real name, Global Custom Commerce, in their press releases and internal communication. That made sense at the time, because the Blinds.com name was instantly understandable to associates, investors, and analysts. Accordingly, everyone at Home Depot thought of us as a blinds retailer. While we were that on the surface, that's not how we viewed ourselves, nor what we considered our greatest value. We knew our talents and opportunities ran much deeper.

But the name "Blinds.com" stuck.

It soon became difficult to get past it and the limitations it put on us. The first impression that name gives is that you sell blinds, and that's all you do. You're not a technology company. You're not a direct marketing company. You're a blinds company.

We didn't like that, so we began a stealth strategy of rebranding in ways that would force the GCC name up the Home Depot ladder. For instance, we created a new, more high-tech logo.

In PowerPoint presentations, we used the GCC blues, more so than the Home Depot orange, although we always acknowledged "a Home Depot company" below the GCC name. We didn't want to be completely autonomous, which would defeat the purpose of being part of Home Depot. That was a huge advantage for us, and we wanted to leverage that. We wanted those at Home Depot to see "Global Custom Commerce, a Home Depot company" and feel good about it.

Every time someone put us on an agenda or discussed us using the Blinds.com name, we corrected them. When we hired and onboarded associates, we shared the story of Global Custom Commerce and our foundation, our culture, our core values, and about being a technology company. It required education frequently and at every meeting.

When I go back to the earliest conversations I had with the leadership of Home Depot after the merger—CEO Frank Blake and founder Bernie Marcus—I was following their guidance in fighting for our true moniker. They wanted us to remain entrepreneurial and visionary. They wanted us to avoid getting pulled into the "big corporate grind," as Frank once described it to me.

It took us six years to finally be known by our real name, but it was worth it. Global Custom Commerce eventually became the Center of Excellence for Configurable Products for Home Depot. To bring back an early lesson, words matter, and, as the leader, you can't sacrifice your brand no matter how tedious and drawn out the battle. Giving up on that name would have meant giving up on our vision for the company.

The 3 Love Languages of Business

The question I am asked most frequently is whether we were able to maintain our culture after the merger. We were, but only after I had an important insight.

In the book *The Discipline of Market Leaders*, authors Michael Treacy and Fred Wiersema write that there are three principal ways companies can lead: Operational Excellence (cost), Customer Intimacy (service), and Product Leadership (innovation). To excel, you must focus mainly on one. It doesn't mean you are only good at one. It's just that you choose one as your dominant operating philosophy.

Home Depot, while caring greatly for its associates, clearly centers on Operational Excellence. GCC, on the other hand, focuses mainly on Customer Intimacy. It's important to understand each perspective and not try to force one to be like the other. *The 5 Love Languages*, by Gary Chapman, espouses the idea that there are five ways to love, and conflict and disappointment from expectations not met can be minimized by not expecting one partner to have the same love language as the other. Home Depot and GCC have different business love languages. It was by understanding this and accepting the differences that we were able to coexist and learn from the other.

INTEGRATION TIPS FOR ACQUIRERS

1. Get aligned early. Discuss and include the target's senior leaders in the integration plan ahead of closing.
2. Don't rush integration; give the target time to get acclimated to their new environment.
3. Integrate only where it makes sense (e.g., HR, Accounting, etc.).
4. Identify the target's secret sauce and let all acquiring associates know it's sacrosanct (know each other's love languages).
5. Have one person as the point of contact.
6. Listen. You might learn something from the new kid on the block.

INTEGRATION TIPS FOR TARGETS

1. Make your numbers so you avoid lots of "outside help."
2. Develop relationships with as many influencers as possible, understand their objectives, and discover ways you can help them achieve theirs.
3. Speak up respectfully any time decisions are being made that have existential ramifications.
4. Understand each other's love languages.
5. Don't whine; grow up. You're now in the big leagues.
6. Listen. You will learn a lot.

Those Reins Aren't Yours Forever

If you've built something lasting, it will outlive you, or at least your leadership. That's the goal and the measure that you've succeeded. Your company can and will live on without you.

If that isn't a clear possibility, you will have trouble selling your company. A business that relies heavily on one or two people has significant vulnerability and an artificially short life span—yours. In the long-term vision, this is a key reason why delegation to form an effective team is so important early on.

Most buyers assume the value of a company will decline if its leader leaves too quickly. They want to know you will not leave right after the deal closes and make matters worse by taking people with you. Naturally, buyers want continuity so what they are purchasing will continue to exist.

On the other hand, nobody wants to buy a business that is dependent on any one person. It's the tricky dance an entrepreneur must perform in negotiations. Convince them you want to stay past selling, but that your presence is not necessary.

It's one of the reasons Home Depot chose us.

"There was an outfit in Colorado that we looked at," Kevin said. "They were never going to be more than blinds. They were just looking for a check, and then they were going to bail. Then I'd have to convince Home Depot people to move to Colorado and take care of it. That's never easy because they think they're leaving the mothership to go work on some weird thing."

As a seller, you want all cash, and if you can get it, of course take it. However, most buyers want to give you enough to make you happy but incentivize you to stay. Try to find other ways to convince them of your sincere interest in continuing to lead your company.

I made it clear to Home Depot that my long-term vision of extending our technology platform to other hard-to-buy product categories was still a dream that had not yet been realized and this partnership was the missing link. They had the existing product categories, veteran merchants, supply chain, retail operations, and customers. We could become Home Depot's Center of Excellence for Configurable Products. It was the perfect match, or so it seemed to me—unfortunately, as I've discussed, most others at Home Depot did not agree. But this was not just an opportunity for me to cash out and jump ship. Still, my investors and I needed Home Depot to show us their commitment and belief in our value as a partner—and that meant money.

So, while an acquirer doesn't want you to leave right away, they do want the security of a succession plan.

Three years after the merger, Home Depot and I both got what we wanted in the form of Steve O'Connor. Steve had worked for Home Depot in Atlanta for nine years, then left for four years to become an executive for a service provider to the company. In that respect, he knew their culture but was not technically an inside man.

At the time, I had pegged someone else I hoped would succeed me, who was talented and smart. Businesses are fluid and nimble, and it was during this time that the direction of who would succeed me evolved.

Home Depot sent Steve to us to be our temporary CFO, something I was wary of at the time, surmising he'd been sent to integrate us into their culture and to micromanage our finances. To control us. Or that he'd make seemingly innocuous changes, which might ultimately lead to unintended consequences that could eventually erode everything.

However, I quickly came to understand how necessary Steve was to our successful integration and how deeply he cared about protecting what we had built. We integrated where it made sense, including human resources, and pushed back where it didn't, such as the way we built our technology. We had been using agile development as a methodology for years, ever since we'd developed Autobahn, and it had worked very well for us. With over $100 billion in revenue, Home Depot has lots to lose, so like many large companies, they were careful to think things through before doing any work. There was simply no way we were going to use a "let's think of every single tiny detail before we do anything" approach.

"The plan was to work there for about a year and a half. Home Depot thought, 'You know us well, you know what we do is amazing, but you know we can jack things up. And we have this acquisition we just bought that we don't want to jack up,'" Steve said. "'They have a great culture, they do amazing things, so where it makes sense, we should integrate. But at the same time, don't let us break them.'"

Steve not only integrated our company with Home Depot, but himself into the GCC culture. So much so that after his eighteen months were up, I asked him to stay. At first, similar to Steve Riddell, he demurred. Conversely, he noted that he needed to be challenged and that staying in the finance role indefinitely wouldn't teach him anything new. Still, I asked him to be my successor and was thrilled when he accepted.

"He understood the value as far as connectivity to the mothership. And that I viewed this place as home. I was here to protect it. I was learning every day from him," Steve said.

Perhaps the most important part of decision-making and problem solving, and where I have been able to coach my leadership team the most, is listening. For example, when Steve joined us, he had to make a radical shift in the way he had operated for most of his career. At the corporations he came from, such as GE, his value had been in forcing staff to conform to the established rhythm of the operation. At GCC, if it hasn't been made abundantly clear already, we encourage vigorous debate, but not in the form of conformation. We want our people to create their own rhythm, which yields more innovative solutions.

Steve added, "When I first got here, I was trying to drive integration with Home Depot where it made sense to me. People in the building would push back, and I would run over them, because I'm well trained to do so. It was a very directive approach. They'd be talking, and I talked right over them. I had to shut it down. Jay taught me how to influence through listening and asking good open-ended questions, rather than talking."

Eventually, I stopped leading SayJays, and Steve took over. I attended fewer senior leadership meetings, so they got used to me not being there. It's confusing for associates when it appears there are two bosses, so I kept my presence to a minimum. When I had questions, I often filtered them through Steve.

"This is one of the things that usually kills a startup or small business—when the charismatic founder starts to move on and we don't have succession planning done," noted Kevin Hofmann.

Establishing and openly promoting our succession plan was a critical part of what made the merger, and my ultimate departure, successful.

SMART WITH MONEY, SMARTER WITH PEOPLE

The Huge Payback of Authentic Generosity

Be a warrior when it comes to delivering on your ambitions.
And a saint when it comes to treating people with respect,
modeling generosity, and showing up with outright love.
—Robin S. Sharma

While I was on my way out of GCC—slowly, but surely—I spent a lot of time thinking about my people, my team over the years, and how I'd strived to interact with and lead them. There are a lot of things that come to mind, but a word that stands out really clearly that I haven't yet sufficiently emphasized is *generosity*. There are many different kinds of generosity and many different ways to be generous with your team. A company-wide pizza party is one small, obvious gift, but I like to think deeper than that and, as always, to look further down the line. This means that something generous you do for your team or an individual associate—such as encouraging them to figure a problem out on their own, or not hand-holding when self-accountability provides the better outcome—might take some time to emerge as the truly generous act that it was. But it will emerge, and it will create more value in your relationships with your associates over time.

As a leader, I've found that generosity is key—and it must be true generosity. So, this is not a chapter detailing the ways to *appear* generous, while at the same time conserving cash and delivering a fat bottom line. That is a strategy that your associates will see right through. Being generous means truly wanting what's in your team's best interests so in return you will get what you want and your business needs: engaged associates who reciprocate by doing their best without ever being told to do so.

We had an associate, one of my all-time best, who was a rising star but lacked genuine empathy for his direct reports. A career blocker. I noticed him going through the motions of *acting* like he cared, but it rang hollow and not just to me. In one of our one-to-one monthly discussions, I asked him point blank, "Are you doing that because you want people to do what you ask, or are you doing it because you truly care?"

I believe my candor shocked him, but I'd made my point.

After that meeting, I noticed him begin to demonstrate real compassion and generosity, and many others told me they noticed, too. Had we not had that conversation, it would have been unfair to him—a disservice. He later left GCC to become the cofounder and CEO of a well-financed, ambitious startup.

In my past, I'd been hesitant to have such direct, hard conversations. But I learned that if you don't, no one reaches their full potential, including you. Yes, generosity with your associates likely will lead to greater profits and productivity, but that is not, and should never be, the point. It's a happy by-product.

Be generous with people because it is the greatest opportunity a person in power can have. Focusing on helping people, no matter the ultimate mission of the company, creates positive returns far beyond a boost to sales and talent retention.

You've seen throughout this book many examples of investments in people through training, time, feedback, and compensation. All are important, and one type of generosity cannot compensate for the others. For instance, if you refuse someone the time they need to help a family member, but you pay them well, you have simply given them golden handcuffs.

Take, for instance, the story of Marissa Franklin, who started with GCC in 2012 in Sales as a Design Consultant. She told me this story in an email eight years later, when she heard my departure was imminent.

"I was in training for just a few weeks, and I was so excited/nervous because we were about to get on the phones," she wrote. "That Sunday night, right after the company Christmas party, my two-year-old niece died very tragically in a drunk driving accident. My family and I were completely broken at that moment, and there was no way I could make it into work the next day. I was going to need to help my sister through planning the funeral arrangements.

"I told myself, 'There goes your job.' Surely they will fire me because I'd be coming off as unreliable so soon.

"Early Monday morning I called HR and explained what happened, and the company made me feel at peace, knowing I could take the time I needed. I knew at that moment that Blinds.com was very different from any other place I had worked.

"I returned to work a week later, and, to my surprise, Kevin Barrios, the head of HR, let me know Blinds.com would pay me bereavement leave while I was out. I can't tell you how much this meant, because I had spent all my savings to help my family pay for funeral costs. This was one of the most difficult times in my life. I can't put into words how your company has impacted my life and how much I appreciate the people who have worked here."

Generosity means knowing what your people need individually when they need it. Even before they know they need it. Not through some divine clairvoyance but through honest communication. They need to feel comfortable telling you what they need, to trust that they can express themselves without fear of judgment or retribution. It doesn't mean you always give your associates what they seek—that's not always possible or in the best interest of your business—but perhaps you can find another way to lighten their load or shore up their resources or mentor them to think differently or ask better questions.

Just the act of communicating as people and not as employer to employee is a form of generosity. Remove the cubicles and titles, and simply communicate with each other. Let them know through your culture, words, and behavior that they are important to you and they can be honest. That's our **Express Yourself** core value—live it every day and it will allow you to see the type of generosity each team member needs.

For Steve O'Connor, active listening and coaching is the generosity I could offer him. His time as an executive in major corporations, including General Electric, had many managers with a highly directive leadership style using fear-driven motivation. When he joined GCC, he saw how differently we did things.

"I kick my heels every morning going to work, and at this stage of my career, I didn't ever think I'd be saying that. I don't fear if I make a mistake. I have to do my job. I have to hit my numbers, but I don't fear the repercussions of making a bad decision."

Loyalty Makes You Family

For Seth Todd, who wants to one day run his own company, generosity means giving him the latitude to lead in his own way. That's why he was willing to take over the new exploratory growth R&D division, part of our ambidextrous organization, although it meant leading a much smaller team initially.

"One of the agreements we had was my business didn't have to be run the way the rest of the business has to be, because we were trying to do something completely different," Seth said of his time leading that department. "So, to some degree, he said, 'Do whatever you want.' For me to have the backing of an actual organization and not have to do this in terms of a startup, where I'm begging somebody for $20 every week, was pretty amazing.

"We literally got to say how we wanted to do things. We've had an opportunity to test completely different organizational structures and what might be feasible, and some of that has even proliferated its way into Home Depot. For instance, we have a rule that you can't have a standing meeting on the calendar. The reason for that is because if there's nothing to talk about, I don't want $200,000 worth of labor coming up with some stuff to say just because there is a meeting on the calendar."

What happens at most large companies is you have an issue and need someone else's help—let's call that person Joe. Your executive assistant calls Joe's executive assistant, but Joe's not available until next

Thursday. You need to include two or three other people in the meeting, so everyone moves schedules around to find a compatible date, most likely one or two weeks out. Then you meet, talk about it, and maybe solve the problem. A lot of time goes by and nothing's been done.

"You can see how that snowballs," Seth said. "One project we did when we started cost roughly $3 million and was done in twelve months. In a large company, something like that might have cost $7.5 million and taken three years. It's the small things that make you able to do that. If you've got a problem, and someone needs to help you solve that problem, you go find that person right now. Jay was willing to let us go do that and mess around with it until it worked. And it does work."

Of course, generosity brings a tremendous return on investment in terms of employee retention, loyalty, productivity, and more. But again, that personal benefit can't be the motivation. You must truly care about your people. You must choose generosity when no one is looking. Like picking up garbage, if you only do it when someone is looking, associates will feel the disingenuity.

For example, when we merged with Home Depot, it was paramount to me that everyone in the company would benefit. I could not face my associates, who had given so much to me, and tell them I was now financially secure and I wish them luck with their new corporate overlords. So I made sure they all got stock options. And that they vested instantly when we merged. Home Depot was also keen on ensuring the options vested. They even made it a condition of closing. One of Home Depot's eight core values is *Taking Care of People*, which they certainly did in our case.

"That was why I left Reliant Energy, so I could have some part of the company," Daniel said. "It was a huge driver for me."

After the merger, I took some of my own money and gave each of my 175 associates enough to invest in either a 529 education account if they had children, or an IRA. I required each person to individually tell me which they were choosing and why, giving them my own advice when they asked, and I handed them a personal check. Generosity here was not just about the money, or I would have cut them each a check with no strings attached. This was also about educating my associates on financial planning for their families. It was one of the highlights of my career when each associate came into my office and offered how, in some cases, their gift helped change their life. One associate, Chris, with tears of joy, asked if he could use it to pay for medications for his mom and, of course, I said yes.

At the same time, as part of the merger, I had a retention pool I could distribute to executives over either a two-year or three-year period. I chose two, which may seem counterintuitive *if* you're thinking only about business. Theoretically, if I spread it out over three years, I could have kept those executives longer. But I wasn't completely sure what I had gotten them into and I didn't know if they were going to be happy. I did not want them stuck at GCC waiting another year, disillusioned and unmotivated, working half-heartedly. I did tell them what I'd done. If you're going to provide a benefit, you need to communicate it, or, to the recipient, it has no value.

Besides ensuring that my associates benefited financially from the merger, and actually felt like they had, I gave Daniel, Larry, Marilynne, Houston, and Steve fine watches tailored to their personalities, from a Breitling Navitimer chronograph for Larry to use during his skydives to a Jaeger Reverso for Daniel due to his ability to see things from multiple perspectives. The lesson here is not just about showing appreciation, but that every person is different, and leaders need to be attentive to each person's differences.

Interestingly, my gift-giving ability doesn't apply to my personal life. My family will not let me forget the time I gave my daughter, Esther, a car battery charger for a white elephant Chanukah gift. The fact that

Lead from the Core

I still don't understand why that gift was so terrible indicates I'll never get it right.

The decision to be generous to the team helped because we didn't lose a single associate until almost three years after the merger.

You Heard the Frugal Part, Right?

Although I try to be generous with people, my business model is fiscally conservative. That may not be evident by the abundance of free food in our office, Ping-Pong table, game room, or the custom video game for which I paid $50,000 so associates and guests could play it, but I have always looked for ways to keep expenses low.

Way back when, I paid $1,500 to build the Lauras.com website and $3,000 for NoBrainerBlinds.com's, and I used a borrowed computer. In The Alley, Ann's desk was a door laid down across two filing cabinets. For more than seven years, I kept track of all my sales manually on lined memo pads, which, in retrospect, was pretty silly. After a while, I was doing it out of superstition as much as fiscal responsibility.

One way to keep costs down is to be a strong negotiator. There's really no trick to it. The key is simply to make sure the other party wants something more than you do. Go into the discussion with that mindset, knowing that if you don't get it, everything's going to be fine. If you push too hard, people will feel it, and you will agree to things you shouldn't.

It's also critical to know what the other party wants. Ask questions to find out what they're really trying to achieve; then you can usually figure out something that will get you both to the path of what you want. Maybe give up something that is less important to you, but because it is important to them, they feel like a victor.

Go into negotiations with fallback positions. The authors of *Getting to Yes: Negotiating Agreement Without Giving In*, Roger Fisher and

William L. Ury, called it BATNA: Best Alternative to a Negotiated Agreement. For instance, if you want one thing in particular, have a fallback that is an acceptable outcome. If you just get that, that's a good start. And the next time, you might get even more.

This mindset is also important whenever you go into a meeting, such as a sales presentation. Know precisely what you want to achieve, but have predetermined second-best alternatives. And third best. Even a fourth. This is the only way you'll know if your meeting was successful: by defining success in advance.

"At the time Home Depot purchased us, we were deep in discussions with Lowe's," Daniel said. "But Lowe's had this very strict general counsel who wanted to push a lot of liability onto us, and we were at an impasse. But we didn't want to shut down the deal, so it was on the slow burner. Meanwhile, Home Depot is shopping for somebody, and got scared Lowe's was going to get us instead. I think Home Depot came in expecting to buy some technology tools, some configurator, a website, a cheap acquisition.

"Jay is a masterful storyteller. He thinks about it for hours, about the drama of what should be the beginning, what should be the end, how to mix in emotion in a real way. So they came in here and got the whole story. And they had starry eyes, and thought, 'Whatever it is about this company, we've got to get it for the influence it's going to have on Home Depot.'

"We sold them the idea, which we really believed in, that we're going to be custom everything, not just a blinds company. That was really effective in getting them interested in a larger purchase price."

Never go into negotiations thinking it's a zero-sum game. These are people you're likely going to deal with later, and they need to trust you. Whatever you negotiate, if you say you're going to do it, you'd better do it. Build a reputation of trust, a reputation of doing what you say you're going to do. Be a person of principled reputation, always. Don't be a jerk.

The Schmuck Factor

There is a consistent theory among many Americans, helped along by TV and movies, that CEOs, especially the more successful ones, are not nice people. They believe leadership is about bossing people around.

My daughter, Esther, felt so strongly about this erroneous theory that she started a website in 2009, NotAllCEOsAreJerks.com. Her site highlighted C-level executives who gave back to their communities and participated in interesting or extraordinary activities. That's how Esther got into the public relations business and expanded her marketing role for the company as our in-house PR manager. It's also how I began to think about this book and the lessons on how to be a human entrepreneur who leads from core values.

If you are, or through your great success become, someone who is not nice to other people, it will hurt you in business. No matter what you read or hear about entrepreneurs, it is not necessary to treat people badly. The choice is yours.

Take for example, my first acquisition, Blindswholesale.com. That purchase came with the ability to rent (i.e., license) the Blinds.com domain name, which was owned by a man named James Katz. When I realized I needed to own the domain name, I made a deal I was very happy with to purchase it. That part you know. What I haven't told you yet is that someone had actually offered James *more* money than I did to purchase Blinds.com. Unfortunately for that fellow, the way I perceived him was the popular opinion—as a real jerk. As much as others didn't like him, James liked him even less.

"I'm not selling it to that jerk," James told me during our negotiation. "I want to sell it to you just so he doesn't get it."

Then there was the time I was working at Meineke Mufflers. Sam Meineke was soft-spoken and mild-mannered, and despite being a multimillionaire, he always dressed casually in jeans and a short-sleeved shirt. One day, as Sam did each day, he arrived at the office after visiting the post office, where he retrieved multiple large canvas bags filled with franchisee reports and franchise fee checks. Sam literally brought in the cash. A new employee saw Sam, thought he was the mail assistant, and asked him to mail a letter for her. Without flinching, Sam said "Sure!" and walked off with the letter. I don't think Sam thought twice about it, but I've thought about it frequently.

Here are some tips to keep in mind to prevent yourself and those around you from losing sight of how to be a good human and a tough competitor.

TIPS ON NOT BEING A JERK

1. Manage your stress so you're emotionally even.
2. Don't make assumptions, but test people's assertions.
3. Do not allow yelling by anyone.
4. Engage in minimal sarcasm.
5. Do not micromanage. Give people autonomy.
6. Believe people really can surpass their own expectations; let them know that; and then provide them the resources and tools to do so.
7. Have very few rules. I'd prefer our employee handbook be one sentence: "Do what's in the best long-term interest of the company and all the stakeholders in it."
8. Be as generous as possible.

Please Speak Louder

Our third core value, **Express Yourself**, was originally Encourage Individual Expression, but people weren't clear on my intention. They thought it just meant that they were free to wear whatever clothes they wanted, which, while I'm also fine with that, missed the bigger point. Seth said it best:

"What it really means is that we pay for your brainpower, that mental capital you have. And if you don't give it to us, then it's wasted money. We expect you to be yourself; we expect you to provide that perspective. And we expect you, as a leader, to create an environment where that's not something that requires repercussion.

"Most large companies have an environment where if you speak up against the wrong person, you're going to pay for it. Whereas here, anything you have to say, you say it, we'll have an argument about it, we'll fight about it, we'll argue about it, but it's never going to be a personal attack. It's going to be about the issue."

8 REASONS WHY PEOPLE DON'T SPEAK UP

1. People see it as not worth the effort. A previous poor supervisor who took feedback but never acted on it.
2. They fear retaliation.
3. They fear looking stupid.
4. They have been taught never to challenge authority, believing it is always good politics to agree with your boss.
5. People are afraid of speaking in public, or culturally taught not to do so.

6. They haven't developed skills for giving candid feedback.
7. There is no upside incentive.
8. Your door isn't really open. Asking people to give you feedback and being available to take it are not the same. Make sure that when you say your door is open, you really mean it! Even better, don't mention that your "door is open," but instead say that you'll come to them!

I've learned in recent years that encouraging people to speak up does not guarantee the diverse perspectives we need. While I've never cared whether a candidate was male or female or of any particular background, if I believe that we want everyone to speak up so we have access to unique perspectives, then I need to deliberately hire people who likely have different views and come at situations in different ways. To do that requires consciously making decisions that provide a more diverse workforce.

I appreciate the way philosopher Michael Marder elevates diversity in *The Philosopher's Plant: An Intellectual Herbarium*, in which he says, "Assuming that two blades of grass were completely identical, they would have represented one perspective, one life . . . one blade of grass . . . In that case, the world would be poorer—or, better yet, it would *not be*—since it flourishes only in and as the variance among the beings that comprise it."

If you hire for diversity, you must support diversity as part of your culture, too. If you truly want to help someone become better than they ever dreamed possible, you have to believe in them and make sure that is a nonnegotiable part of your culture. It's one of the things our top Design Consultant, Dixie, appreciates most about GCC:

9 WAYS TO ENCOURAGE SPEAKING UP

1. Tell people you want feedback and ask for it frequently. Make public examples of good cases to honor those who speak up, so that others understand that the trust is there should they feel the need to come to you.
2. Practice the basics of active listening, including repeating parts of the conversation back to them. Don't just wait for your turn to speak.
3. Put your cell phone down for the conversation and close your laptop.
4. Reciprocate in an equally candid way. Explain the merits of the idea and ask questions about things that may cause barriers, rather than being dismissive.
5. Respond quickly even if you need time to think about it.
6. Be available. If you're always out of the office, in meetings, or in a closed room, the feedback will not reach you. Everyone should be encouraged to contact you by whatever means necessary, whether it's email, phone, or in person.
7. Allow people to communicate in private—in writing or in person.
8. Let people know your plans for their input, even if you've decided not to do anything.
9. Thank them.

"We celebrate Pride Day every year, because Jay wants people to know he loves everyone and that you should be the best of who you are.

We have a transgender associate who had only worked here for about six months, and on Pride Day he got on the microphone and said he never thought he could work for a company that would truly support him. Not only that, but Home Depot supports transgender surgery, so this individual can really become the man he wants to be.

"To me, that's huge. It brings tears to my eyes when I can see someone's life truly affected by just the simple fact that they work here. I don't think there's a lot of places you can truly have that support. If you want to wear your pajamas to work, if you want to work from home, if you want to wear your leotards every day, if you want to wear your baseball cap every day, however it is that you want to look, you can look, and that's important when you dedicate so much of your time to your job. And the people you work with become your family. It's so good to be somewhere where you feel comfortable in whatever skin you're in."

GCC has always been highly diverse, but don't mistake diversity for inclusivity. You can hire diverse associates, but part of **Evolve Continuously** is making sure all associates feel welcome and appreciated and heard.

It's OK to make mistakes, and if you have a culture of **Express Yourself**, your team will let you know when you have missed the mark. That happened to us once when we planned a company event for associates and their families at a local establishment called The Redneck Country Club. The person in charge of planning the event was not from this country and did not understand the racist history of the Confederate flag, which was conspicuous on the property. Our African American associates were incensed—and rightfully so.

We immediately spoke with the associates who were upset, and cancelled the venue, losing a $35,000 deposit, which I consider to be absolutely worth it. Had it not been for a close association with our team, this unwitting mistake might have escalated into something messy. We fixed it and learned from our mistake.

As I said, GCC has always been highly diverse—but not always so among our senior leadership team, which I knew was something that could not continue. In 2014, we hired Marcia Porchia, initially as Director of Project Management, and later promoted to Vice President of Accountability and an official member of our senior leadership team (SLT). She is the first African American member of GCC's SLT and the second woman after Marilynne Franks Bleeker, our former Director of Accounting.

"It was big," Marcia told me about her joining the SLT. "It created a connectedness [with associates] unlike before because, until then, the females and minorities never saw anyone in leadership that looked like them."

Since adding Marcia, GCC's nine-person SLT shifted to include four women and three people of color.

Marcia formed a Diversity & Inclusion Committee that has been effective at celebrating Hispanic Heritage Month, International Day, Gay Pride Week, and Black History Month, and encouraging associates at SayJays to share their culture, along with food, of course, specific to the region. It's created comfort between constituencies.

As part of its charter, the D&I Committee states: "At GCC, our goal is to attract, develop, and retain the best and brightest people from all walks of life and backgrounds. This requires our organization to have the right culture of inclusion where all individuals feel respected, are treated fairly, provided work-life balance, and an opportunity to excel in their chosen careers."

That statement was brought into the light after the murder of George Floyd on national TV, followed by days and months of riots throughout the country in the summer of 2020. I called Steve O'Connor and Marcia in July of that year to discuss how the associates were handling the situation.

"I don't think anything really prepared us for what we saw with George Floyd and then the emotions that carried forward afterwards, not only by the external world, but our own associates," Steve said, adding, "Even though we have a core value to express your views, people are comfortable enough to do it sometimes at work on work-related stuff, but there are certain topics that people have been taught since they're two years old that you just don't bring into the workplace."

CEOs have frequently asked my advice as to whether they should take a stand. I can't give anyone an answer to that question, but I will say this: It's understandable to avoid political issues at work. It's understandable not to take an open position on your political views as a leader—to do so may promote an environment that is not inclusive. But be careful what you classify as "political." Some things are simply about right and wrong. The right cultures do more than yield higher profits. They yield higher moral authority.

"When things like this happen in the country and you have a certain group of people, and it's not just African American people, who feel overwhelmed by what they see and how they feel they've been treated, it's very hard to turn that emotion off when you transition from outside of work to work," Marcia said. "What this also does is it really sheds light on the fact that sometimes the conversations with an associate are very superficial. It's not just about this topic, it could be about something happening in someone's family. What we're finding is leaders just aren't having conversations with their associates to really understand what's going on with them, period. It's really about leaders engaging with their associates and understanding where they are in life, so if adjustments need to be made to help them be more successful at work, they can be."

HOW TO COMMUNICATE DURING POLITICALLY AND SOCIALLY SENSITIVE TIMES

1. Whether you expressly take a stand or not, either way you're taking a stand.
2. If you do not say something, your views will be assumed by others—and likely far from your real views.
3. Use your core values to guide what you say and how you behave. If candor is a core value, be candid.
4. Whatever you do say, if it doesn't ring true, all your other views will now be suspect.

Be honest with yourself. A core value of **Express Yourself** can only go as far as you allow it to. You and your leadership team define the boundaries of any value like that every single day, with every conversation you start, end, engage in, or walk away from. You tell your associates what is appropriate to bring to work by what you choose to express about yourself.

Marcia and Steve saw that our core value of **Express Yourself** had room to evolve, to move beyond work-related opinions and into truly expressing one's identity and challenges and expectations.

"You always said that the number one responsibility of a leader is to develop their people," Steve told me. "I would add to that: and to ensure they build relationships with their people to make them feel comfortable to be able to speak up, that they build relationships and a safe working environment that allow for those conversations."

Of course, there's a flip side to this ultimate value of **Express Yourself**. We value expressing oneself with candor and respect, so is it hypocritical to prevent some topics from being discussed? Big-ticket items might be obvious, but things that some might consider innocuous might be extremely distracting, triggering, or offensive to others.

For instance, we used to restrict employees from selling Girl Scout cookies and raffle tickets, promoting charities, and discussing political views in the workplace. Over time we realized that it was indeed hypocritical. How could people trust that they were really able to express themselves if there were specific things that were off limits? The main consideration, now, is that these things of course may be freely expressed, but it cannot get in the way of doing business. It's also true that even if you do not verbally express something, what you might see as a harmless sign, holiday decoration, or slogan posted up in your work area might feel like harassment to others.

Who's Ready for a Promotion?

Being generous with people doesn't remove their accountability to earn increased responsibilities and roles. In fact, not holding them accountable for their own self-improvement does a very ungenerous disservice to them in the long run.

Here's a question I really dislike hearing: "So, when am I up for my next promotion?"

If I hear this question, I've failed to do my job in communicating that the responsibility to get promoted rests with the associates, not me. Your associates must own their own growth in their personal and professional lives. And you, as their leader, have an obligation to provide resources, training, opportunity, and the proper environment to do so.

Avoid the organizational hierarchy and develop a company culture that's about associates creating their own space within the organization. Here are a few tips I give my managers to help guide their team members (and themselves) in identifying a career path.

The first is to treat your career as a sponge, not a ladder. A ladder implies the process is linear, straight, and has an immediate next step. Instead, think of your career as a sponge that gets bigger and more valuable as you soak in increased levels of responsibility, experience, and influence. The second is not to base your personal success path on those around you. No two careers are alike, just as no two associates are exactly alike. Gather best practices from the successes around you and help all those around you do the same.

Are you doing all that you could? When I hear an associate express a desire to transition to another role, the first thing I want to know is what they're doing about it. Are they staying on top of industry trends? Are they volunteering to create content or help with special projects to grow relationships and obtain new skills? Are they reading, taking classes, watching webinars, and otherwise growing themselves? A career jump is easier and more successful if you've built yourself a bridge.

6 WAYS TO HELP GET YOURSELF PROMOTED

1. Ask your supervisor if you can assume some of their work, which eventually will either show that you are ready to take on higher levels of responsibility, or will morph your existing job into a higher level of responsibility. Then you have earned the right for higher pay.
2. View your career as a sponge, not a ladder, soaking in best practices from others.

3. Do not base your personal success on those around you, because no two careers are alike and no two people are alike. Instead, base your success on how you compare to your prior self.

4. Aggressively study the role you desire.

5. Acquaint yourself with other departments' work, create contacts there, and learn about what they do. You might surprise yourself to learn there are positions that excite you that you'd never imagined. Volunteer to assume some of that work.

6. Get creative. Understand where you excel, then think how you might use that excellence to help the company in ways no one had ever imagined. An example is Brad, who began his career in Customer Service, but because of his passion for video, developed and managed all of our internal communication digital media boards.

The Iliad Comes Before the Odyssey

Before your team can embark on your vision, they need the skills to help them get where they're going. And when you have an organization that requires evolution constantly, you had better give associates a way to evolve, not just tell them to do it.

One of the greatest gifts you can give someone is knowledge. Help your associates garner new skills, on your tab, and do so without worrying about where they will take those skills. They very well may end up working for a competitor, using abilities you helped them obtain.

But you don't create and keep a great team by limiting their ability to grow. You do it, as this chapter's theme has shown, through generosity.

We formally instituted that practice of arming our associates with as much knowledge as possible when we created the Institute for Learning, Innovation, Advancement, and Development, or the ILIAD. This talent development and learning center at GCC is focused on designing and delivering learning solutions that enrich our associates' knowledge. We launched the ILIAD in 2017, three years after the merger. Home Depot cares about its associates' growth, too, but we needed something tailored to our specific objectives, such as disruptive agile thinking, for a company of our specific size and level of development.

In addition to demonstrating to associates that we were investing in them, the ILIAD transformed the way we onboarded. Before, we'd trained new associates through lecturing, going through notes, asking questions, having tests—it was boring and ineffective and took a long time. The ILIAD was initiated by our Chief People Officer and eventually headed by Marcia Porchia. As a result, our learning became more engaging, more interactive, more experiential, and more effective. It transformed the way all of our associates learned.

And it wasn't just for new hires. There were offerings for existing leaders, those who wanted to become a leader, or those whom we had identified as having leadership potential. We observed our gaps as a company, then offered training to fill them in, like leadership development, talent management, how to facilitate and coach ownership thinking versus accountability, business basics, growth and career blueprints, and so on.

We held annual leadership summits and promoted them heavily to associates. It was expected that all associates who had at least one direct report would participate. We sometimes brought in outside professional speakers, but the best part of the summits was that our own leaders did the training. One of the management masters of all time, the late Andy Grove, former CEO of Intel, strongly asserts in his book *High Output*

Management that it is the manager's role to train. Our involvement gave us a chance to showcase our personalities and expertise, and, even better, we probably learned more than our associates by crystallizing our thoughts and collaborating to make the team more effective.

Investing in our people and their development was a critical testament to GCC's belief in continuous evolution, although it's important to let your associates know the ultimate responsibility for their improvement rests primarily with *them*. We frequently reminded them of this. The responsibility of the leader is to honestly coach and mentor their associates to help them make those self-determinations of their weaknesses and strengths, to take the appropriate classes, engage in them, and decide on their career paths. It's an integral part of how we help them become better than they ever dreamed possible.

HALF FULL AND HALF EMPTY

The Secret to Simultaneously Dealing with Disparate Dilemmas

*The test of a first-rate intelligence is the ability to
hold two opposed ideas in the mind at the same
time, and still retain the ability to function.*

—F. Scott Fitzgerald

There are many things about me and my leadership style that seem at odds with each other. And that is a critical component of my success—and likely yours, whether you know it or not. On the one hand, I advocate **Experiment Without Fear of Failure**. However, I am risk averse. You won't find me anytime soon jumping out of an airplane to see if I can figure out how to fly on the way down. I take pleasure in asymmetric risks, or those that present a more significant upside than down.

Perpetually, the best way to overcome the fear of experimentation is to find that downside risk: if you can live with that, there is nothing to fear.

That's one of the reasons I prepare extensively before meetings. I don't wing it. My commitment to no surprises works both ways. I don't blindside others and I work hard to ensure the same is true for me. No one likes surprises and it breeds distrust. If people don't trust you, you can't amount to anything.

I prepare for any big meeting by asking people beforehand for their questions so I can prepare my answers. For presentations, I ask knowledgeable people who are familiar with my projects to poke holes in my content. I want to know what's faulty, unclear, and deficient.

The more input you get, the better you will be, as long as you listen to it. You must swallow your ego and accept as much help as you can get. And yet, you must be able to discern when advice doesn't feel right. Throughout your career, you'll get a lot of guidance, and much of it will be contradictory. Listen carefully, review the data, then throw it out and do what you think is right. You must live with your decisions. The worst thing is to do something you intuitively think is wrong, even if the experts tell you otherwise.

With a Grain of Salt

Even the advice you get in this book is suspect. What's worked for me are not necessarily the things that will work for you. We all have strengths and weaknesses, and varying personal traits, all of which influence us. And don't forget luck and timing. Yes, you can make your own luck, but sometimes you just happen to be in the right place at the right time—which, really, is its own form of luck.

That's why the core value **Express Yourself** is not just lip service. You want people who approach problems from diverse perspectives to speak up, so you can gather as much data as possible before deciding.

In another example of paradox, I'm both an introvert and an extrovert. Some would assume I'm entirely an introvert, given that I spend most of my time in the office. On the other hand, I've performed in the same barbershop quartet for over forty years, and I love to perform in front of an audience, including taking on numerous speaking engagements.

The truth is, I'm both. I once took a test that revealed I'm 51 percent one and 49 percent the other—I can't remember which, but it doesn't matter. I can be extroverted when needed and tap the calm and focus of an introvert. They both exist in me, and knowing that about myself is helpful.

26 PARADOXES FOR SUCCESSFUL LEADERS

1. Keep the ultimate vision in mind; take dead aim on today's task.
2. Be experimental and risk averse.
3. Knowing you will be better tomorrow provides comfort in where you are today.
4. Vulnerability is strength.
5. The more impossible something seems, the more enticing it is to try.
6. The attempt to avoid failure makes failure more likely.
7. The less you know about a topic, the more likely you'll come up with a novel idea about it.
8. Learn from your competitors; play your own game.
9. Leverage your strengths, but taken to an extreme, they become weaknesses.
10. Every department has numbers to optimize; optimizing them does not optimize the entire organization.
11. Iterate on your core; take stair-step initiatives for your future.

12. Business is serious stuff; enjoy the ride.

13. To know the future, learn the past; for future effectiveness, unlearn the past.

14. Extroverts make great leaders; introverts make great leaders.

15. The more weaknesses you discover, the happier you become, because you now have the ability to improve more.

16. Delegate as much as possible; you're ultimately responsible.

17. Build your confidence by first succeeding in small ways; tackle the most daunting obstacle first because if you can't solve it, all the time and money you spent on the small stuff will be wasted.

18. The more structure you have, the more spontaneous you can be.

19. Budgets and plans are necessary; plans stifle thinking big.

20. Have several uncorrelated paths to your objectives; focus on one.

21. The fewer decisions you must make, the more decisions you can make.

22. Everyone must be treated equally; treating people identically is insensitive, disrespectful, and sometimes unfair.

23. The more formidable your expertise, the less luck you need; the more formidable your expertise, the luckier you get that someone else will notice and provide you with more opportunities.

24. Learn how to tell vivid, motivating stories; get right to the point.

25. Provide consistent, ample training so your people do not become stagnant, get bored, and then quit; boosting your people's skills makes them valuable to other companies, increasing the likelihood they will leave to join those other companies.

26. Feel sad for the death of loved ones; delight in life.

Don't Retire, Rewire

My passion for GCC led some to believe I would leave immediately after the acquisition, while it led others to think I wouldn't go through with the sale in the first place.

"I never thought Jay would sell. He loved the company so much," Home Depot's vice-president Mike Mahler said immediately after the acquisition.

Of course I loved the company—still do. But I also knew I couldn't stay there forever. When loss has become a frequent companion in your life, it may be easier to embrace experimenting without fear. You've lost the things that mean the most to you in the world, and yet you survived—and even flourished in some ways.

That's what gave me the confidence to make one of the pivotal decisions of my life. It was very difficult to announce I was leaving GCC, which I did on December 12, 2019. I had already handed over much of the day-to-day operations and decision-making, and Steve O'Connor was clearly the heir apparent, which gave the team comfort and time to get to know him.

When we merged, I knew it was just a matter of time before I'd leave, although I had no idea how long. I figured I'd stay at least three years, because there was that much work I needed to do. Others thought I would leave right away.

For example, six years after the merger, just before Carol Tomé, Home Depot's then CFO, left and later became CEO at UPS, I asked her point blank, "How long did you think I was going to stay?" Without pause, she said, "We thought you would hate us and leave after a month."

I told her that it had been a slow, steady process of weaning myself from the company, going all the way back to 2001 when I first bought BlindsWholesale and gave up 40 percent of my company. Afterward, it was raising institutional capital, replete with covenants and restrictions with the objective of selling one day. All those years of answering questions and taking heat from my investors and reporting to a seasoned board primed me for the role of subordinating and inoculating myself from the frustrations usually associated with accepting a subservient role from new owners.

When you build something, irrespective of the amount of money you get for selling it, you still feel responsible for its well-being. Your legacy is your company. And you want the foundation and culture you've built to be instilled into the new leadership.

Setting up how and when I would leave became another way I minded the gap. The first condition I needed to know before leaving was that my successor had been determined and that I, and anyone at Home Depot who needed to, had approved him or her. I personally spoke with each person I knew would have to make that approval and asked them directly, "Steve's approved, right?" and I looked them in the eye and waited until they said, "Yes."

The second thing I wanted was to make sure Autobahn was going to be used for more than blinds, and that GCC was dubbed, officially, the Center of Excellence for Configurable Products for hard-to-buy solutions. So, I had a meeting with Home Depot CEO Craig Menear a few weeks before I made the final decision to leave. He assured me GCC was in fact the Center of Excellence for Configurables.

Then there were some organizational design and people changes that needed to be made, and I wanted to see those through, including replacing GCC's Chief People Officer. I wanted to guide the new person to ensure the culture and values we had created would be maintained and not somehow be usurped by what might be a more hierarchical perspective.

Finally, I needed to make sure the company was no longer dependent on me and, equally important, I was no longer psychologically dependent on it. I had removed myself from a lot of meetings and the roof didn't collapse. In fact, we did great. So, I began to plan my next steps.

Barbara always described my daily commute as "going to my playground," and she was right. There was never a day I didn't look forward to being in the office. So, naturally, Barbara was concerned that my identity was so completely wrapped up in my CEO role that I might struggle with retirement from GCC.

She might have had a point there if I had intended to retire. That was never part of the plan. I did not intend to slow down, nor retire. I was going to rewire.

I never wanted to leave the business world. It's fun for me, and I can provide value. I wanted to teach, so several weeks before I made the announcement, I became an entrepreneur-in-residence professor instructing graduate students at Rice University's Jones Graduate School of Business and began mentoring at my alma mater, The University of Texas at Austin, also serving on UT's advisory board at the Herb Kelleher Entrepreneurship Center. I joined some startup advisory boards, and later two public company boards, as well as not-for-profit boards. Before leaving GCC, I began doing many of the things I wanted to do after GCC. So, when the day came for me to leave, my rewirement was already in motion.

People have asked me if I ever had any regrets after making the announcement. Never. I was happy with the plans I had made for life post–Home Depot. A big part of that life is my family. My seven grandchildren—I call them my seven startups—and perhaps more. The work I could do with them, and my adult children, the influence I could have over them, was far more important than the influence I could have with any business. And, of course, much more time with Barbara, including traveling the world.

Barbara; Esther; Esther's husband, Doug; and their two children, Naomi, six, and Tova, four (their third child, Austin, had not yet been born), were there when I told my associates I was leaving. All the GCC associates were able to see me with them and to see how happy-go-lucky and sweet they are. I think that gave a lot of people peace of mind that I would be OK. It certainly helped me through the announcement, having some of my main motivations literally staring me in the face.

Barbara and I are compatible in so many ways. The way we both worked together with our grandchildren was another foundational reason for my equanimity. We'd also be able to travel together and serve our communities without the constraints of running a business. The sale was certainly a marker of what we'd built, but the financial independence it gave Barbara and me to be together wherever and whenever we wanted, especially with our children, grandchildren, extended family, and friends, was the most important facet.

Like our acquisition announcement, my rewirement declaration happened at a SayJay, and only a few people knew in advance. I gave Home Depot the eight months' advance notice they had requested. The announcement was made in December at our holiday party, with a departure date of May 1, 2020, which meant associates had almost another half-year with me, which gave them comfort. Steve O'Connor, the senior leadership team, and my executive assistant, Shannon, knew, as well as a few people within the company whom I had worked with for many years and had a special relationship with.

When it came time to make the big announcement, it took me three weeks to think of what I wanted to say. I described our history and invoked the names of those who had been a key part of the GCC journey. I counted our successes and milestones, touching on each of them with care and gratitude.

I reminded our team that we now represented the preponderance of blinds sold online. A market leader usually has 35 percent of market share—and I made it clear that the success wasn't mine.

"Everything we've done, all our success, is because of our culture—our **4 Es**: **Evolve Continuously**, **Experiment Without Fear of Failure**, **Express Yourself**, and **Enjoy the Ride**. Our ability to win comes from our core values," I said.

I had to separate myself from the ability of the company to succeed. I had to wean them from whatever belief they had that I was integral to the company. After a lifetime of work to build, nurture, and grow it, I had to tell these people it could live without me. It could grow without me.

The hardest part, and in part why it took until six years after the acquisition for me to leave, was that in order to say this to them, I had to believe it myself. I could never tell them something I didn't believe.

I told them, "It's about you evolving. That's what's made us successful."

Ironically, the video of my rewirement announcement is proof that our core values could sustain the company without me. If you watch it now, the first moment or two is audio without video. That's because the team recording the announcement had a technical difficulty and missed the first couple minutes of the SayJay.

When I found out, I was distressed. It was a pinnacle moment in my life. How could they miss that? However, the team experimented without fear of failure and created a slideshow of photos of me in the early days of GCC. The video starts with a compelling visual history of the company we built together with my audio as the voice-over. They didn't ask me. They just solved the problem, and it turned out better than I had ever dreamed possible.

All of it did.

WHAT FOUNDERS SHOULD CONSIDER BEFORE STEPPING AWAY

1. Ensure your key principles for success are embedded in everything and everyone.
2. Have your successor in place prior to leaving and get your direct reports accustomed to following him or her so that you wean them from your involvement.
3. Give the apparent successor time with your team without your presence and help get them acclimated to their new boss, because it's hard for people to report to two bosses.
4. Stay attuned to what people are saying by having one-on-one discussions.
5. Ensure that any pet projects of yours are completed, or well on their way to completion, with a key sponsor tasked with finishing each of them.
6. Have your next gig determined in advance and, if possible, begin it while still at your current role, which, if you do everything above, will diminish the time needed at your current job.
7. Give ample notice; give hints years in advance that one day you'll be gone.

Not All Leaders Are Jerks, but We Are All Human

One paradox with which many leaders struggle is empowering decision-making among a leadership team, while also ensuring the job gets done right.

What I've learned, sometimes painfully, is you give people as much latitude as possible to do their jobs, but still inspect quality. I've made the mistake of not inspecting enough. Some years ago, someone at a high level on my leadership team took advantage of the trust I had in him, as well as an organizational gap he saw after the merger. He did not turn in an expense report for nearly two years.

Signals got crossed between the folks at Home Depot and me, so no one was checking the reports. We each thought the other was doing it, but instead, he was going directly to someone in Payables, who assumed, since he was a senior leader, that he was allowed to spend without approval. As you can guess, changes were made.

Another paradox: I'm very impatient. I will push as fast as I can to get something done. But if we're not getting there immediately, I've learned to be patient and wait. Still, I don't let it go; I continue to watch it, nurture it, coax it along, and wait for it to grow in the right time. For example, although I knew very quickly after meeting Barbara that I wanted to marry her, I knew with patience, marriage would come at the right time for all and be a better union for it. It's the collision of wanting more but also being happy in the moment. As a leader, that is a critical balance to find.

My definition of success is "being in the process of improving myself and everyone within my sphere of influence." The more I find in myself that's deficient, the more opportunity I have to evolve. Most run themselves down judging their personal deficiencies. Knowing that you will get better and that you will not be in the place you are now makes you comfortable being in the place you are now. That in turn leads to taking fast actions, which leads to yet another paradox I learned from businessman Naval Ravikant: "Be impatient with the actions you take, but patient with results."

Just discovering and admitting that something is wrong is in itself a type of improvement. There are enough people who will tell you you're no good or can't do something. If you incrementally improve, be grateful and know there's still so much to do, for which you should also be grateful. That's what I felt the most the day I finally walked away from GCC, a company Naomi and I birthed at the same time, and Barbara helped me raise: gratitude. I was so thankful for the journey and all the individuals who agreed to go on it with me. I believe that came through in my parting email to associates:

How grateful and lucky I've been for 24 years to have built something out of nothing and affected so many people's lives. Seeing my associates grow from entry level positions to formidable leaders. And even those who left us to start their own businesses, lead other ventures as CEOs and senior VPs, or discovered and cultivated a new skill to be used elsewhere in a more satisfying way—nothing is more fulfilling.

We focused first on helping people become better than they ever believed possible, and financial success then ensued. Our behaviors were guided by our 4 core values. The 4 E's: (1) Evolve Continuously, (2) Experiment Without Fear of Failure, (3) Express Yourself, and (4) Enjoy the Ride!

And those values will continue to propel my life's trajectory into the next phase. So, it's not retirement; it's re-wirement.

Tomorrow I have the blessing of complete peace of mind, knowing that my child is in expert hands, with a team fully capable and highly motivated to do everything we've ever dreamed of doing—without me.

Thanks for the opportunity to be consequential.

At the same time, there were many instances over the years at Say-Jays and other gatherings when I shared how proud I was of a team accomplishment or when I related a story about Naomi, and allowed myself to be emotional in that moment, to be genuine and trust that my associates accepted me as the human I am. It helped that in my loss of Naomi, Barbara's compassion for me, and my family, was always present, and still is today. That takes a heart filled with generosity, and Barbara's allowed me to feel safe to express such vulnerability.

In turn, I always did the same for them.

As a leader, you must be tough and kind at the same time. Be tough on profit, be tough on growing your business, but always be kind to people. That means it's kinder to help someone realize that not being in the company might be better for them. One associate was told such, and upon leaving became a successful CEO elsewhere.

The same goes with humor and having fun. There are so many things in our office that are there merely because they amused me or someone else on our team, such as fuzzy dice hanging from the ceiling in the conference room named *the Van*. There are many wonderful memories I have along this journey that didn't add to our bottom line in any way, but made us happier. At this stage in my life, **Enjoy the Ride** is my favorite core value because I understand it more fully now than ever before.

What's interesting about fun is that research has shown that people seem to be more authentic, and can be more conceptual and creative, when they're having fun and at ease. When you push people too hard to perform, they actually perform worse. And they certainly do not do any more than they're told. Loosen up.

One night I met the conductor of the Houston Symphony Orchestra, Andrés Orozco-Estrada, after a concert performance. I asked him how the musicians were able to smile while they were obviously working so intensely on the music, which had a particularly tricky syncopation. He responded, "The harder the piece, the more they enjoy playing it."

Life's Big Little Secret

Your company must perform in the same world of paradoxes. As Jim Collins writes in *Good to Great*, great companies have a set of core values and a purpose that do not change, and yet, great companies change relentlessly. They evolve strategies and processes, and sometimes people, to adapt with the times.

Great companies do both. Great companies know the difference.

Channeling my inner Collins, I told my associates during my rewirement announcement, "Great organizations transcend any single idea or product. Great organizations transcend any single invention. And great organizations transcend any single individual. The best organizations are not dependent, even on their founder. GCC is not dependent on *me*. It's dependent on *you*."

Here's the ultimate paradox: I have not owned a majority of GCC for over fifteen years. When I retired, I didn't own a single share. But it has always been my company, and in my heart, it always will be. If you can replicate that feeling within yourself and your team, you will be successful.

The paradox I have had to reconcile the most in my life is how to be sad about my mother's and Naomi's deaths and happy about how my life turned out. When I realized I could have both feelings simultaneously, life started to make more sense.

IT'S NEVER TOO LATE

*Life itself is a race, marked by a start, and a finish. It is what
we learn during the race, and how we apply it, that determines
whether our participation has had particular value.*

—Ferdinand Porsche

Grief and happiness are not mutually exclusive. The two can coexist, like acidity and sweetness in wine. Sometimes, the joy is even greater because of the grief, but the combination is inevitable in life.

I have been able to share that lesson with others who are grieving, including one of our associates. Being able to help someone in their hardest moment is a great blessing.

He had worked for us for a few years. Then, his significant other unexpectedly died from unknown causes—it was hard to tell what had happened. He was one of our top salespeople, and he was a strong athlete, but after she died, he withered away. It was hard to look at him. He didn't come into the office for two years. When he came back, I saw him at a meeting and gave him a hug.

Later, he asked me, "How did you do it?" meaning how did I move on after losing Naomi.

I told him, "The fact that you are sad means you loved her and that you had a great relationship. It's OK to be sad. It *is* sad. Don't try to figure out how not to be sad."

He later told me that giving him permission to be sad changed his life. Nobody had ever said that to him, that it was fine to be sad.

My son Craig believes it was the loss of his mother that pushed me to become the leader I am.

"I'm not sure he would have the same level of success if my mom hadn't died. I feel like that moment changed him so much," Craig said. "From that growth, he was able to learn how to be a leader."

Just a few days before Naomi's death, she laughed and told me, "I know you're going to be successful, get remarried, and have the big house."

It was so hard for me to hear that, to think about any future that didn't include her.

Even with death hovering near, she never let go of her humor and love, which had been a constant through our marriage. I keep both of those traits at hand still, in everything I do, and with them, her spirit.

The glass is half empty *and* half full. You must accept that and be thankful there's anything in it at all.

Take my advice, don't take my advice, but no matter what, **Enjoy the Ride**!

ACKNOWLEDGMENTS

I began writing this book with about the same amount of experience I had when starting my business. None.

So it was incumbent on me to reach out to others to help guide me. And in most cases, have them do the work I'd never be able to do as well as they. What a treat and privilege it's been to collaborate and marvel at the work of so many people, whether it was in business when Daniel Cotlar insightfully analyzed data, then took the right actions; or, for this book, with Joseph Galantino's masterful shading techniques in his illustrations, and my numerous editors who magically reorganized chapter sections for clarity, or simply changed the tense of a verb or removed a comma—just to give a few examples.

I am grateful and appreciate all of you for your skills and insistence on the highest quality you can muster. In addition to those talents one could easily observe, there was another talent that must be acknowledged. It was the talent to artfully *express* yourselves to help the business, book, and others to *evolve*.

Many of you worked behind the scenes and are not mentioned in the book, so these acknowledgments are to ensure your impact is publicly recognized.

Each journey starts with a single step. Starting this book started with a single person, Candace Beeke. Thank you for taking disparate bits and pieces of my life, conducting interviews, sifting through my notes and audio files, and writing the nucleus of the book. I always knew you could help me craft the story not only with business aplomb, but also with heartfelt empathy.

Thanks to those who generously devoted their time to edit. Such a diverse group gave me diverse opinions. Just when I thought we were almost finished editing, one of you would offer yet another unique tweak. Of particular importance was how you helped add authenticity, eliminating the sugarcoating I've been known to do, by reminding me of the angst and dilemmas we faced. The result is a book that depicts the inner anxieties, difficult decisions, and the many prescriptive ways we overcame them.

Thanks sincerely to editors and fact-checkers Johnny Goodman, Shashi Mudunuri, Daniel Cotlar, Larry Hack, Steve Riddell, Marilynne Franks Bleeker, Steve O'Connor, Shannon Campbell, Al Danto, Dr. Katie Pritchett, Todd Jensen, Dr. Luis Martins, Ernie Rapp, Rachel Stout, Alec, Esther, Craig, and Barbara.

My impressive professional publishing team at BenBella Books, headed by Matt Holt, believed in the book right from the start. It includes folks who continually improved the manuscript beyond my expectations. Sincere thanks to Matt, Katie Dickman, Mallory Hyde, Brigid Pearson, and Michael Fedison.

A tip of the hat to Gary Goldsmith, for partnering with me in high school on my first business, filling a pain in the marketplace (i.e., custom T-shirts for the many sports teams we together coached), and providing early proof that business is fun.

Then there were those of you who helped just because you're that kind of person. Thank you for your generosity, wisdom, tips, referrals, encouragement, and reinforcement. Thanks to Scott Sonenshein, Stu Diamond, Tom Waite, Dick Eiger, Ann Tanenbaum, Carol Edelman (who has also watched over me for almost fifty years), Bob Buday, Ed Winthrop, Martin Lindenberg, Mark Goulston, Michael Treacy, Dottie DeHart, David Schmerler, Avinash Kaushik, Michael Benson, Rita McGrath, Katie Laird, and Carl Dyer (for providing me with the physical and mental stamina to write).

To my kids, I'm sorry.

To good luck, I couldn't have done it without you.

For all of you, this experiment is *our* book.

I hope you enjoyed the ride.

INDEX

Index

Index

Index

Index

Index

Index

ABOUT THE AUTHOR

Jay Steinfeld founded and was the CEO of Global Custom Commerce, which operates the world's number one online window covering retailer, Blinds.com. Launched in 1993 for just $3000 from his Bellaire, Texas, garage, Global Custom Commerce was acquired by The Home Depot in 2014. Jay remained as its CEO and later joined The Home Depot Online Leadership Team. After stepping away from these roles in early 2020, he has increased his involvement on numerous private company boards and serves as a director of the public company Masonite (NYSE: DOOR). He also teaches entrepreneurship at Rice University's Jones Graduate School of Business and supports numerous charities.

Jay is an Ernst & Young Entrepreneur of the Year and has earned a Lifetime Achievement Award from the Houston Technology Center. Active as an industry speaker on topics including corporate culture, core values, how to scale a start-up, and disruption, he has more than 100 published articles. He also sings in the same barbershop quartet of which he's been a part for nearly fifty years.

He lives with his wife, Barbara, in Houston, Texas, and has five children and seven grandchildren, whom he proudly refers to as his *seven start-ups*.

Visit Jay at www.jaysteinfeld.com.